BIBLE CHARACTERS
FROM THE
NEW TESTAMENT

Volume 1

"Blessed are they that have not seen, and yet have believed."

6

BIBLE CHARACTERS
FROM THE
NEW TESTAMENT

VOLUME 1:
Joseph and Mary to James,
the Lord's Brother

ALEXANDER WHYTE, D.D.

Introduction by DAVID R. MAINS

Illustrations by RON McCARTY

KEATS PUBLISHING, INC. NEW CANAAN, CONNECTICUT

**BIBLE CHARACTERS FROM THE NEW TESTAMENT, Volume 1:
Joseph and Mary to James, the Lord's Brother**

Shepherd Illustrated Classic Edition published 1981

This volume previously appeared as the fourth volume in the
six-volume series, *Bible Characters*, published by Oliphants
Ltd. of Edinburgh and London

Library of Congress Catalog Card Number: 81-81099
ISBN: 0-87983-256-8

Printed in the United States of America

SHEPHERD ILLUSTRATED CLASSICS are published by
Keats Publishing, Inc.
36 Grove Street, New Canaan, Connecticut 06840

CONTENTS

ILLUSTRATIONS

INTRODUCTION TO THE SHEPHERD ILLUSTRATED CLASSIC EDITION

In seminary, the Chapel messages of one particular professor stirred me so that it was impossible to do anything but spend the next hours in quiet, by myself, pacing back and forth across the campus. The obvious priority at the moment was to sort through the deep, insistent voice of the Spirit. Classes were cut, meals forgotten, all other obligations abandoned.

Even today, after hearing exceptionally good sermons, I prefer to be alone with my thoughts—but unfortunately, encounters like these seem to be extremely rare.

I'm told that in this day when teaching seems to dominate our pulpits, a revival is occurring regarding preaching. If there is a return of good preaching that touches the heart, I predict the sermons of Dr. Alexander Whyte will be in even greater demand. These two volumes of collected messages demonstrate his exceptional gifts.

I strongly recommend that these pages be read aloud. In other words, "preach them to yourself." Hear the flow of the words. See how pacing enhances good delivery. Learn how intellect and emotion complement one another. Most importantly, give the Holy Spirit opportunity to enter these century-old sentences

. . . exhortations, and to speak powerfully to the heart.

I also suggest reading aloud only one character study each time. These strong sermons were not conceived to be quickly absorbed, then followed immediately by another. Much of the impact of Whyte's words will be found in the private silence you purposely create for yourself after each chapter. Fortunately, you, the reader, can make that significant pause a possibility.

More than once, I have found myself stirred, needing quiet, reflectively walking back and forth across the campus of my life. As you sit under Whyte's ministry through these pages, you will also begin to appreciate several ways in which he was uniquely skilled. The most obvious of these is through the preacher's sanctified imagination.

In his sermon on John the Apostle, he cautions, "Do not be afraid at the word 'imagination', my brethren. It has been sadly ill-used, both name and thing. But it is a noble name and a noble thing. There is nothing so noble in all that is within us. Our outward eye is the noblest of all our outward organs, and our inward eye is the noblest of all our inward organs. And its noblest use is to be filled full of Jesus Christ, as John's inward eye was."

In his *Bible Characters*, Whyte's imaginative skills amaze and delight. Time and again, you are convinced he must have known these people personally, and if not these specific men and women, then certainly he understood human nature intimately well.

Only at first, and then just occasionally, the suspicion rises that he might be pushing things too far—his imagination is too clever. But soon you become confident that Whyte's inner eye consistently picked up these warning signals as quickly as you do. As you read and listen to him more, you relax, because this gift is very much under the Spirit's control.

Whyte also uses humor—original, never excessive, but the wryness is definitely there; he experiments with various formats—he has a unique style, but his creativity refuses to be reduced to formula preaching; he has a charming way of mixing present and past— " 'I actually have the name of Simon Magus on my communion role,' Philip telegraphed to Jerusalem"; and lastly, he employs that hard-to-capture but wonderfully pleasing element of surprise.

There are other benefits to be derived from a closer relationship with this man. Alexander Whyte is a "wordsmith." There's a rhythm to the way he uses words in his sermons. Oh, that we might read them aloud with a Scottish accent!

The careful, scholarly side of his personality is also obvious in his preaching. How enlightening to be able to share his familiarity with Bunyan, Dante, Teresa, the Puritans and a host of others. Whyte's love of books was not merely for self-satisfaction; to him, they were tools to use in communicating God's truth.

I personally find his style of intertwining Scriptures very satisfying. While discoursing about one individual, Whyte has a subtle method of making the whole of Scripture dance before your eyes. Reading these sermons makes this technique more apparent then attempting to explain it.

Pay particular attention to Whyte's sermon introductions. He is adept at quickly capturing his listeners. Here is a brief two-sentence example:

"Our men of natural science are able sometimes to reconstruct the shape and the size of a completely extinct species from a single bone, or splinter of a bone, that has been quite accidentally dug out of the earth. And in something of the same way Pilate's wife rises up before us out of a single sentence in Matthew's Gospel."

Did you catch the surprise element as well?

Finally, I must mention his skill at application. It was said that to go and hear Dr. Whyte preach was to take your life in your hands. May God give us more men like this in our pulpits!

This skill as much as any is why I am anxious that these pages not be used as occasional private devotional readings. They are too strong. Don't misunderstand, they are filled with devotion, if in your mind that word carries thoughts of earnest devotedness, religious fervor and great concern; but these are much more than just interesting character studies of two handy volumes in which one can grab some quick insight for help with tomorrow's Sunday School lesson.

Treated properly, they represent the incredible privilege to privately visit a different time and place and hear one of the finest of God's servants preach once again under His anointing. To do so is not to be entertained, although the experience can be extremely satisfying. "He's good! In fact, very good!" you will exclaim.

But it's the Voice behind the voice you'll not want to miss.

Approached properly, that communication miracle can easily be yours. The Spirit can actually reveal your character to you through these pages. This must be the real test of greatness in a preacher: Is God freed to speak?

For years the people of Edinburgh sat under the preaching of Dr. Alexander Whyte. I invite you now, through these pages, to do likewise.

Come, take your life in your hands!

David R. Mains
November, 1981

BIBLE CHARACTERS
FROM THE
NEW TESTAMENT

Volume 1

BIBLE CHARACTERS

LXX

JOSEPH AND MARY

SAINT MATTHEW and Saint Luke, the first and the third Evangelists, tell us all that we are told of Mary. They tell us that she was the espoused wife of Joseph a carpenter of Nazareth, and that the Divine Call came to her after her espousal to Joseph and before her marriage. What a call it was, and what a prospect it opened up! No sooner was Mary left alone of the angel than she began to realise something of what had been appointed her, and what she must now prepare herself to pass through. The sharp sword that the aged Simeon afterwards spoke of with such passion was already whetted, and was fast approaching her devoted and exposed heart. On a thousand sacred canvases throughout Christendom we are shown the angel of the annunciation presenting Mary with a branch of lily as an emblem of her beauty and as a seal of her purity. But why has no spiritual artist stained the whiteness of the lily with the red blood of a broken heart? For no sooner had the transfiguring light of the angel's presence faded

from her sight than a deep and awful darkness
began to fall upon Joseph's espoused wife. Surely
if ever a suffering soul had to seek all its righteousness and all its strength in God alone, it was the
soul of the Virgin Mary in those terrible days that
followed the annunciation. Blessed among women
as all the time she was; unblemished in soul and
in body like the paschal lamb as she was; like the
paschal lamb also she was set apart to be a divine
sacrifice, and to have a sword thrust through her
heart. Mary must have passed through many dark
and dreadful days when all she had given her to
lean upon would seem like a broken reed. Hail,
thou that art highly favoured of the Lord, the angel
had said to her. But all that would seem but so
many mocking words to her as she saw nothing
before her but an open shame, and, it might well
be, an outcast's death. And, so fearfully and
wonderfully are we made, and so fearful and wonderful was the way in which the Word was made flesh,
that who can tell how all this may have borne on
Him who was bone of her bone, and flesh of her
flesh; to whom Mary was in all things a mother, as
He was in all things to her a son. For,

Hers was the face that unto Christ had most resemblance.

Great is the mystery of godliness: God manifest in
the flesh. A man of sorrows, and acquainted with
grief. These are the beginnings of sorrows.

Joseph's part in all this is told us by Saint
Matthew alone. And as we read that Evangelist's
particular account of that time, we see how sharp

that sword was which pierced Joseph's soul also. His heart was broken with this terrible trial, but there was only one course left open to him. Conclude the marriage he could not, but neither could he consent to make Mary a public example, and there was only left to him the sad step of revoking the contract and putting her away privately. Joseph's heart must have been torn in two. For Mary had been the woman of all women to him. She had been in his eyes the lily among thorns. And now to have to treat her like a poisonous weed —the thought of it drove him mad. Oh, why is it that whosoever comes at all near Jesus Christ has always to drink such a cup of sorrow? Truly they who are brother or sister or mother to Him must take up their cross daily. These are they who go up through great tribulation.

What a journey that must have been of Mary from Nazareth to Hebron, and occupied with what thoughts. Mary's way would lead her through Jerusalem. She may have crossed Olivet as the sun was setting. She may have knelt at even in Gethsemane. She may have turned aside to look on the city from Calvary. What a heavy heart she must have carried through all these scenes as she went into the hill country with haste. Only two, out of God, knew the truth about Mary; an angel in heaven, and her own heart on earth. And thus it was that she fled to the mountains of Judah, hoping to find there an aged kinswoman of hers who would receive her word and would somewhat understand her case. As she stumbled on drunk with sorrow

Mary must have recalled and repeated many blessed scriptures, well known to her indeed, but till then little understood. "Commit thy way unto the Lord; trust also in Him, and He will bring it to pass; and He shall bring forth thy righteousness as the light, and thy judgment as the noonday. Thou shalt keep them in the secret of thy presence from the pride of men; thou shalt keep them in a pavilion from the strife of tongues." Such a pavilion Mary sought and for a season found in the remote and retired household of Zacharias and Elizabeth.

It is to the meeting of Mary and Elizabeth that we owe the Magnificat, the last Old Testament psalm, and the first New Testament hymn, "My soul doth magnify the Lord, and my spirit hath rejoiced in God my Saviour." We cannot enter into all Mary's thoughts as she sang that spiritual song, any more than she could in her day enter into all our thoughts as we sing it. For, noble melody as her Magnificat is, it draws its deepest tones from a time that was still to come. The spirit of Christian prophecy moved her to utter it, but the noblest and fullest prophecy concerning Christ fell far short of the evangelical fulfilment.

She is a happy maiden who has a mother or a motherly friend much experienced in the ways of the human heart to whom she can tell all her anxieties; a wise, tender, much-experienced counsellor, such as Naomi was to Ruth, and Elizabeth to Mary. Was the Virgin an orphan, or was Mary's mother such a woman that Mary could have opened her heart to any stranger rather than to her? Be

that as it may, Mary found a true mother in
Elizabeth of Hebron. Many a holy hour the two
women spent together sitting under the terebinths
that overhung the dumb Zacharias's secluded house.
And, if at any time their faith wavered and the
thing seemed impossible, was not Zacharias beside
them with his sealed lips and his writing table, a
living witness to the goodness and severity of God?
How Mary and Elizabeth would stagger and reason
and rebuke and comfort one another, now laughing
like Sarah, now singing like Hannah, let loving and
confiding and pious women tell.

Sweet as it is to linger in Hebron beside Mary
and Elizabeth, our hearts are always drawn back
to Joseph in his unspeakable agony. The absent
are dear, just as the dead are perfect. And Mary's
dear image became to Joseph dearer still when he
could no longer see her face or hear her voice.
Nazareth was empty to Joseph; it was worse than
empty, it was a city of sepulchres in which he
sought for death and could not find it. Day after
day, week after week, Joseph's misery increased, and
when, as his wont was, he went up to the synagogue
on the Sabbath day, that only made him feel his
loneliness and his misery all the more. Mary's
sweet presence had often made the holy place still
more holy to him, and her voice in the Psalms
had been to him as when an angel sings. On one
of those Sabbaths which the exiled Virgin was
spending at Hebron Joseph went up again to the
sanctuary in Nazareth seeking to hide his great
grief with God. And this, I feel sure, was the

Scripture appointed to be read in the synagogue that day : " Ask thee a sign of the Lord thy God ; ask it either in the depth, or in the height above. Therefore the Lord Himself shall give you a sign : Behold, a virgin shall conceive, and bear a son, and shall call his name Immanuel." Joseph's heart was absolutely overwhelmed within him as he listened to that astounding Scripture. Never had ear or heart of man heard these amazing words as Joseph heard them that day. And then, when he laid himself down to sleep that night, his pillow became like a stone under his head. Not that he was cast out ; but he had cast out another, and she the best of God's creatures. Ay, and she perhaps—how shall he whisper it even to himself at midnight— the virgin-mother of Immanuel ! A better mother he could not have. So speaking to himself till he was terrified at his own thoughts, weary with another week's lonely labour, and aged with many weeks' agony and despair, Joseph fell asleep. Then a thing was secretly brought to him, and his ear received a little thereof. There was silence, and he heard a voice saying to him, " Joseph, thou son of David, fear not to take unto thee Mary thy wife, for that which is conceived in her is of the Holy Ghost." Gabriel was sent to reassure Joseph's despairing heart, to demand the consummation of the broken-off marriage, and to announce the In-carnation of the Son of God. Did Joseph arise before daybreak and set out for Hebron to bring his outcast home ? There is room to believe that he did. If he did, the two angel-chastened men must have had their own thoughts and counsels together even as the two chosen women had. And as Joseph talked with Zacharias through his writing table, he must have felt that dumbness, and even death itself, would be but a light punishment for such unbelief and such cruelty as his. But all this, and all that they had passed through since the angel came to Zacharias at the altar, only made the re-betrothal of Joseph and Mary the sweeter and the holier, with the aged priest acting more than the part of a father, and Elizabeth acting more than the part of a mother.

For my own part, I do not know the gift or the grace or the virtue any woman ever had that I could safely deny to Mary. The divine congruity compels me to believe that all that could be received or attained or exercised by any woman would be granted beforehand, and all but without measure, to her who was so miraculously to bear, and so intimately and influentially to nurture and instruct, the Holy Child. We must give Mary her promised due. We must not allow ourselves to entertain a grudge against the mother of our Lord because some enthusiasts for her have given her more than her due. There is no fear of our thinking too much either of Mary's maidenly virtues, or of her motherly duties and experiences. The Holy Ghost in guiding the researches of Luke, and in superintending the composition of the Third Gospel, especially signalises the depth and the piety and the peace of Mary's mind. At the angel's salutation she did not swoon nor cry out. She did not rush either into terror on the one hand or into transport on the other. But like the heavenly-minded maiden she was, she cast in her mind what manner of salutation this should be. And later on, when all who heard it were wondering at the testimony of the shepherds, it is instructively added that Mary kept all these things and pondered them in her heart. And yet again, when another twelve years have passed by, we find the same Evangelist still pointing out the same distinguishing feature of Mary's saintly character, "They understood not the saying which Jesus spake unto them; but His mother kept all these savings in her heart."

And, again, if we are to apply this sure principle to Mary's case, "according to your faith so be it unto you," then Mary must surely wear the crown as the mother of all them who believe on her Son. If Abraham's faith has made him the father of all them who believe, surely Mary's faith entitles her to be called their mother. If the converse of our Lord's words holds true, that no mighty work is done where there is unbelief: if we may safely reason that where there has been a mighty work done there must have been a corresponding and a co-operating faith; then I do not think we can easily overestimate the measure of Mary's faith. If this was the greatest work ever wrought by the power and the grace of Almighty God among the children of men, and if Mary's faith entered into it at all, then how great her faith must have been! Elizabeth saw with wonder and with worship how great it was. She saw the unparalleled grace that had come to Mary, and she had humility and magnanimity enough to acknowledge it. "Blessed art thou among women : Blessed is she that believeth, for there shall be a performance of those things which were told her from the Lord." "Blessed is she that believeth," said Elizabeth, no doubt with some sad thoughts about herself and about her dumb husband sitting beside her. "Blessed is the womb that bare Thee," cried on another occasion a nameless but a true woman, as her speech bewrayeth her, "and Blessed be the paps that Thou hast sucked." But our Lord answered her, and said, "Yea, rather, blessed are they that hear the word of God and keep it." And again, "Whosoever shall do the will of My Father in heaven, the same is My brother, and sister, and mother

LXXI

SIMEON

SIMEON was one of the Seventy. Simeon sat in the Jerusalem Chamber of that day. And it fell to the lot of the Old Testament company on which Simeon sat to render the prophet Isaiah out of the Hebrew tongue and into the Greek tongue. All went well for the first six chapters of the evangelical prophet. But when they came to the seventh chapter, and to this verse in that chapter, "Behold, a virgin shall conceive, and bear a son, and shall call his name Immanuel," Simeon at that impossible prophecy threw down his pen and would write no more. 'How shall this be?' demanded Simeon. And with all they could do, the offended scholar would not subscribe his name to the *parthenos* passage that so satisfied and so delighted all the rest. Till in anger he threw down his pen and went home to his own house. But at midnight an angel appeared to Simeon, and said to him: 'Simeon, I am Gabriel that stand in the presence of God. And, behold, thou shalt remain in this thy captivity till thou shalt see with thine own eyes the LORD's Christ, made of a woman, and till the virgin's son shall put his little hand into thine aged bosom, and shall there loose thy silver cord.' And it was so. And the same Simeon was just and devout, waiting for the consolation of Israel. And he was still waiting in the temple when his parents brought in the child Jesus, to do for him after the custom of the law. Then he took him up in his arms, and blessed God, and said: "Lord, now lettest Thou Thy servant depart in peace, according to Thy word: for mine eyes have seen Thy salvation."

I can only guess at Simeon's real meaning and whole intention when he said in the temple that day that his waiting eyes had now seen God's salvation. For salvation in that day, as in this day, had as many meanings as there were men's minds. Salvation had the very heavenliest of meanings to one man, and the very earthliest of meanings to another man. To one man in the temple that day the salvation of God meant salvation from Cæsar; while to another man it meant his salvation from himself. To one man it was the tax-gatherer, and to another his own evil heart. And, with all that we are so instructively told about Simeon, still it is not possible to satisfy ourselves as to what, exactly, that aged saint and scripture scholar had in his mind when he said that his eyes had now seen God's salvation. But it is not Simeon and his salvation who is our errand up into this temple to-night. It is ourselves. What, then, is our salvation—yours and mine? When we speak, or hear, or read, or sing about salvation, what exactly do we mean?—if, indeed, we have any meaning at all, or intend to have any. 'My son'

—one of Simeon's sacred colleagues used to say to
his scholars—'My son, the first thing that you will
be examined upon at the day of judgment will be
this: What was the salvation that you pursued
after? What salvation did you study, and teach,
and preach, and yourself seek after when you were
still in time and upon the earth?' How happy will
it be with old Simeon on that terrible day when he
hears this read out over him before men and angels:
"The same man was just and devout, waiting for
the consolation of Israel, and the Holy Ghost was
upon him." "Mine eyes," said Simeon, "have seen
Thy salvation." And Joseph and His mother marvelled at those things which were spoken of Him.

And, being full of the Holy Ghost, Simeon went
on to say: "Behold, this child is set for the fall and
rising again of many in Israel." So He was in
Israel, and so He is still. There are schools and
systems of interpretation of Scripture; there are
schools and systems of philosophy; and of this and
that, in which this prophecy uttered by Simeon that
day, is still being fulfilled. They rise, and they
stand, and they fall, just as they receive or reject
Immanuel. But our question with this Scripture
before us is not about schools and systems of theology
and philosophy, but about our own souls. Has
Mary's Son, then; has God's Son, been a stumbling
stone to me? Or, has He been the one foundation
laid in Zion for me? Has He, to my everlasting
salvation, and to His everlasting praise, lifted me up
from all my falls and made me to stand upon His
righteousness as upon a rock? Simeon himself had

at one time stumbled and been broken on this child,
and on His too great name. But the steps of a
good man are ordered of the Lord, and He delighteth
in his way. Though he fall he shall not be utterly
cast down, for the Lord upholdeth him with His
hand. Now, unto Him that is able to keep you
from falling, and to present you faultless before the
presence of His glory with exceeding joy: to the
only wise God, our Saviour.

"And for a sign that shall be spoken against."
We wonder to hear that. We are shocked to hear
that. We say in amazement at that: What did
He ever say or do that He should be spoken
against by any man? He did the very opposite.
He went about doing and speaking only good.
But that made no difference to those men in that
day who spake so spitefully against Him. Some
spake against Him out of sheer ignorance of Him.
They had never even seen Him. But they spake
against Him in their distant villages as if He had
come and done them and theirs some great injury.
And many who saw Him every day spake against
Him every day, just because they did not understand
Him, and would not take the pains and pay the
price to understand Him and to love Him. Some,
again, were poisoned against Him by what other
people, and people of power, said against Him;
some through envy, and some just because they
had once begun to speak against Him, and could
never give over what they had once begun to do.
And they went on so speaking till they were swept
on to cry, Crucify Him! not knowing what they

were saying, or why. Take good care how you
begin to speak against any man, good or bad. The
chances are that, once you begin it, you will never
be able to give it over. When you have once begun
the devil's work of evil-speaking, he will hold his
hook in your jaws, and will drag you on, and will
give you a stake and an interest in lies and slander,
till it will enrage and exasperate you to hear a single
word of good spoken about your innocent victim.
"Judge not," said our Lord, feeling bitterly how He
was misjudged Himself. And Albert Bengel anno-
tates that in this characteristic way: *sine scientia,
amore, necessitate.* " I spoke not ill of any creature,"
said Teresa, " how little soever it might be. I
scrupulously avoided all approaches to detraction.
I had this rule ever present with me, that I was not
to wish, nor assent to, nor say such things of any
person whatsoever that I would not have them say
of me. Still, for all that, I have a sufficiently strict
account to give to God for the bad example I am
to all about me in some other respects. For one
thing, the very devil himself sometimes fills me
with such a harsh and cruel temper—such a wicked
spirit of anger and hostility at some people—that
I could eat them up and annihilate them." That
was the exact case with the detractors of Jesus
Christ. They had no peace in their hearts, or in
their tongues at Him, till they had eaten Him up
and annihilated Him. This is such a horrible pit
of a world that not even the Son of God Himself
could come down into it, and do the work of God in
it, without being hunted to death by evil tongues.

And with that awful warning, and after nineteen centuries of His grace and truth, no man of any individuality, and talent, and initiative for good, can, to this day, do his proper work without straightway becoming a sign to be spoken against. To this day some of the most Christlike of men among us have been the most written against and spoken against, till such speech and such writing may almost be taken as the seal of God set upon His best servants and upon their best work. "And for a sign that shall be spoken against," said Simeon, as he returned the Holy Child to His mother.

LXXII

ZACHARIAS AND ELIZABETH

IGH up in the hill-country of Judea there dwelt a certain priest named Zacharias with his wife Elizabeth. They were no longer young; they had lived a long and a happy lifetime together. The single shadow that had ever lain upon their serene and saintly life had been this that their house was childless. But all that was now long past—long past and quite forgotten. "For thus saith the Lord to them that choose the things that please me, and take hold of my covenant, even unto them will I give in mine house and within my walls a place and a name better than of sons and of daughters: I will give them an everlasting name, that shall not be cut off." And while the Lord spake thus to them both, Zacharias in his holy office spake thus to Elizabeth: 'Why weepest thou, and why is thy heart grieved? Am not I better to thee than ten sons?' Thus the God of Israel spake to them both, and thus they spake to one another, till Luke is able to record this of them both, that they were both righteous before God, walking in

all the commandments and ordinances of the Lord
blameless.

It is the fulness of time at last. It is at last the
great day on which the New Testament has been
predestinated to open. Zacharias has gone up to
Jerusalem according to his course. The priestly
lot has again been cast and has fallen this time on
Zacharias. He is chosen of God and called upon
to enter the Holy Place, to minister at the altar,
and to make morning and evening intercession for
the sinful people. Never before, in all his long
lifetime, has Zacharias had this awful privilege;
only once in a priest's whole lifetime was this great
office put upon any son of Aaron. Clothed in his
spotless robes, with his head covered and with his
shoes off, this holy man and elect priest disappears
within the golden doors of the Holy Place. As
he enters he sees the golden candlestick, and the
table of shewbread, and the altar of incense. From
that altar there rises the sacred flame that had
been lighted at the pillar of fire in the wilderness,
and which has burned on unconsumed ever since.
Taking his censer full of incense into his hand
Zacharias pours it on the perpetual altar-fire, and
says: Lord, let my prayer come before thee like
this incense; and the lifting up of my hands like the
evening sacrifice! And the whole multitude of the
people were praying without at the time of incense.
And there appeared unto Zacharias an angel of the
Lord standing on the right side of the altar of incense. And when Zacharias saw him he was troubled
and fear fell upon him. But the angel said unto

him: Fear not, Zacharias; for thy prayer is heard
and thy wife Elizabeth shall bear thee a son, and
thou shalt call his name John. And thou shalt
have joy and gladness, and many shall rejoice at his
birth. And many of the children of Israel shall he
turn to the Lord their God: to make ready a people
prepared for the Lord. Then follows Zacharias's
fear, and doubt, and disbelief; and then his deaf-
ness and dumbness; and then the visit of Mary to
the hill-country of Judah, where Zacharias and
Elizabeth had hid themselves; and then the Magnificat, as we call it: and then the birth and the
circumcision of Elizabeth's son; and then the
opening of Zacharias's mouth and the loosening of
his tongue, all wound up with his magnificent Bene-
dictus. A splendid preface to a splendid book!

"They were both righteous before the Lord, and
blameless." This is an excellent instance of the
frank and fearless, if confessedly condescending,
style of Holy Scripture. Holy Scripture has no
hesitation lest it should contradict or stultify itself.
Holy Scripture speaks out its whole heart on each
occasion boldly, and leaves the reconciling and the
harmonising of its strong and sometimes startling
statements to those of its readers who feel a need
and have a liking for such reconciling and harmonising. As a matter of fact that was the widespread
good name and spotless character of Zacharias and
Elizabeth. Zacharias among his brethren in the
priesthood, and Elizabeth among her kinsfolk and
neighbours in Hebron, were both blameless. Holy
Scripture in saying this simply classifies Zacharias

and Elizabeth with Abraham, and with Samuel, and with Job, and with all such Old Testament saints. And if such generous judgments are not so often passed on men and women in New Testament times, that is so for reasons that are very well known to every New Testament mind and heart. And if those noble tributes to Zacharias and Elizabeth stagger and condemn us; if we read of their righteousness and their blamelessness with envy and with despair; what is that envy and what is that despair but two of our finest New Testament graces through which we are being led on to a righteousness and a blamelessness that shall not be economical and of condescension, but shall be true and perfect and everlasting. That righteousness, in short, and that blamelessness of which a New Testament apostle prophesies in these so comforting words: "Nevertheless we, according to His promise, look for new heavens and a new earth, wherein dwelleth righteousness. Wherefore, beloved, seeing that we look for such things, be diligent that ye be found of Him in peace, without spot, and blameless." Blessed are they which do hunger and thirst after righteousness, for they shall be filled.

And the angel said unto him: Fear not, Zacharias: for thy prayer is heard. Had the angel come with that answer forty years before he would have been welcomed and well entertained both by Zacharias and Elizabeth. But he has come too late. 'No,' said Zacharias; 'no. It is far too late. The time is past—long past. The thing is impossible—quite impossible. And, indeed—and let not my lord be angry—it is no longer desirable.' Zacharias had long outlived his prayer for a son. He had long retracted his prayer. He had a thousand times justified the Hearer of prayer for not hearing and not answering his too impatient prayer. He had long ere now seen some very good and sufficient reasons why he and Elizabeth should end their days together. And, even if it were still possible, Zacharias was not willing to be plunged back at this time of day into all the anxieties, and uncertainties, and responsibilities, and dangers he had now for so long left for ever behind him. 'My prayer is not to be heard,' Zacharias had long ago said to himself. 'Let me direct my prayer and look up for far better, and far more sure, and far more steadfast, and far more satisfying things. The will of the Lord be done,' he had said long ago. But behold, to Zacharias's confusion, his prayer has been heard all the time! All these long past years of prayer, and waiting, and ceasing from prayer and turning to other things—all that time Zacharias's answer has been ready before God, and has only been waiting till the best time for the answer to be sent down. Pray on, then, all you postponed and disappointed and impoverished people of God · pray on and faint not. Pray on : for the prayer is far better than the answer. And, besides, your answer may all the time be ready, as Zacharias's answer was. But other people's prayers and other people's providences may be so mixed up with yours that you will have to wait till their prayers, and

their preparations, and their providences are all as
ripe and as ready as yours. The fastest ship in the
British fleet has to wait for the slowest, and that
explains why that fine vessel is not led into battle
and let home to harbour with its full and proper
spoil. Zacharias and Elizabeth were ready long
ago. But Joseph and Mary were not ready; they
were still but new beginners in faith and in prayer,
in righteousness and in blamelessness. And thus
it was that, without knowing why, Zacharias and
Elizabeth and John the Baptist had to wait in the
hill-country of Hebron till Joseph and Mary were
made ready for the Divine predestination and for
their prayer away north in Nazareth.

And Zacharias and Elizabeth hid themselves up
in the hill-country for the next five months. Look
at them. Look at Zacharias with his writing table,
and Elizabeth with her needle. And never one word
spoken between them all that time, only smiles
and tears. What, do you suppose, was Zacharias
doing all that time with no altar to minister at,
and no neighbours to talk to, and no tongue, indeed,
to talk with? "I have no books," said Jacob Behmen,
"but I have myself." And Zacharias had himself.
Zacharias had himself, and the wife of his youth,
who was also the light of his eyes: he had himself
and all those past years of prayer, and waiting, and
resignation, and peace of mind. And then he had
these past overwhelming weeks also. Do you still
ask what Zacharias was doing all that time? Has
your New Testament a margin with readings?
Your so instructive margin, if you will attend to it,

will tell you the very Scriptures over which Zacharias
spent his days and nights all that silent time in
Hebron.   All you have got to do some day, when
you are in the mind, is to consult the margin over
against Zacharias's prophetical song, and you are in
that as good as looking over his shoulder at his
writing table.   You are as good as walking out
alone with him when he goes abroad among the
sunsetting rocks of Judea to wonder, and to praise,
and to pray over Elizabeth and himself and their
unborn son.

Zacharias and Elizabeth were sitting alone with
their own thoughts one day when who should knock
at their door but the Virgin Mary herself all the
way from Nazareth.   Luke takes up his very best
pen as Elizabeth and Mary embrace one another.
He had it all long afterwards from an eye and ear
witness, so that we might know the certainty of all
that took place that day in Zacharias's house up in
the hill-country.   With the embrace and with the
authority of a prophetess Elizabeth saluted Mary,
and said : " Blessed art thou among women, and
blessed is the fruit of thy womb.   And whence is
this to me, that the mother of my Lord should
come to me ? "   What a day ! What a dispensation !
What a meeting !   What a household !   What a
predestination descended on that roof !   What
unsearchable riches !   What great and precious
promises !   What prayers !   What psalms !   What
laughter !   What tears !   And Mary said : " My
soul doth magnify the Lord, and my spirit hath
rejoiced in God my Saviour."   And Mary abode

with Elizabeth about three months, and then returned to her own house.

And it came to pass, that on the eighth day Elizabeth's neighbours and her cousins came to the circumcision of the child; and they called him Zacharias, after the name of his father. But his mother answered and said: " Not so ; but he shall be called John," that is to say, The-Grace-of-God. And they said unto her : "But there is none of thy kindred that is called by that name." And they made signs to his father what he would have the child called, and he asked for his writing table and wrote, saying; "His name is The-Grace-of-God." And they marvelled all. They marvelled all because it was a new name to them, and it offended them to hear it. It was to them an outlandish and an unintelligible name. They had never prayed for a son, or for anything else. They had never been visited of an angel. They had never hid themselves five months. Their husbands had never been struck deaf and dumb for their doubt. No babe had ever leaped in their womb because they were filled with the Holy Ghost. No. None of all their kindred had ever been called by this so stumbling name. Fathers and mothers of new-born children, be like Elizabeth and Zacharias in the naming of your children. Be very bold, if need be, in the naming of your children. Be original and independent in the naming of your children. Be truthful. Be thankful. Be believing. Be hopeful, and be assured. Be not afraid to write an altogether new name in your Family Bible. Go back to your true ancestors for

a name sometimes, and not to those of flesh and
blood only. Fish no more for testaments in the
waters of baptism. Or if for a testament at all,
then secure, as far as your naming of him lies, that
your son shall be an heir of God, and a joint-heir
with the Son of God. Name the name of God over
your son. Name over your son what God has done
for your soul. Name over him some secret of the
Lord with you. Name him something that God
has showed you out of His holy covenant. Elizabeth was very bold. She named her little son after
no man on earth, but, actually, after Almighty
God Himself in heaven. And her husband Zacharias
was of one mind with her in that, as soon as he got
his writing table into his hands. The God-of-all-
Grace was thus made Sponsor and Name-Father to
Elizabeth's only son, who was born of her so out of
all ordinary time. Elizabeth and Mary had spent
three months together since Gabriel's visit to them
both. And all those three months—morning, noon,
and night—when they talked together, it was about
nothing else but about the angel, and his visits, and
his messages. And among other things that they
less talked about to one another than whispered to
themselves, was the naming of their unborn sons.
"Immanuel!" and "Jesus Christ!" Mary would
whisper to herself, with an ever-increasing wonder
and awe at the awful words. While "The-Grace-
of-God" was Elizabeth's holy secret. And, then,
how the two children were born, and how they were
brought up, and how they both justified, and fulfilled, and adorned their new and unheard-of names,

let Luke and his fellow-evangelists say. And they will tell you, to begin with, how John—The-Grace-of-God—grew and waxed strong in spirit, and was in the deserts till the day of his showing unto Israel.

LXXIII

JOHN THE BAPTIST

"WHAT manner of child shall this be!" was the universal exclamation of the whole hill-country of Judea over the birth of John. The old age of Zacharias and Elizabeth: the errand from heaven of Gabriel; the dumbness in judgment of Zacharias; and the strange things that he wrote on his writing table; all that made all who heard of it to exclaim, 'What manner of child, we wonder, shall John, the son of Zacharias and Elizabeth, turn out to be!' And the whole manner and character and service of John's childhood and youth and manhood, down to the day of his death, turned out to be wonderful enough to satisfy the most wonder-loving of Elizabeth's neighbours, both in Jerusalem and in all Judea.

John was in the deserts till the day of his showing unto Israel, so Luke tells us. And from Luke, and from some other trustworthy sources, we can see John for the first thirty years of his sequestered life as well almost as if we ourselves had lived in the very next desert to his deserts. For you must

always remember this about John that he was in the
deserts, and was with the wild beasts, till he began
to be about thirty years of age. He was in those
terrible deserts that lay all around the Dead Sea.
Up and down John wandered, and fasted, and
prayed, where Sodom and Gomorrah had once stood
till the Lord rained fire and brimstone upon all the
inhabitants of those cities, and upon all that grew
upon the ground. And John was clothed with
camel's hair, and with a leathern girdle about his
loins; and he did eat locusts and wild honey. A
terrible man. A man not to come near. The
very bitumen-miners, whom everybody feared, were
afraid of John. It made them sober and civil to
one another when John came down to visit them
in their squalid settlements. It was not that John
was a misanthrope. John was the right opposite
of a misanthrope. It was because all other men
were misanthropes; were hateful, and were hating
one another, that John could not any longer dwell
among them, either in Judea or in Jerusalem, either
in Sodom or Gomorrah. You totally misread and
misunderstand John if you think that it was either
misanthropy or moroseness that made John what
he was. It was simply John's extraordinarily deep
insight into the holy law of God that made him
such a monastic of fasting and self-flagellation and
prayer.

Before his father Zacharias died, and as long as
Elizabeth lived, John had heard things like this at
their lips in family worship every day: "The Lord
shall lay on Him the iniquity of us all. He shall

be stricken, smitten of God, and afflicted. His soul
shall be made an offering for sin." It was on such
things as these that Elizabeth suckled her heaven-
sent son till it sometimes seemed to him in his
loneliness of soul and in his agony of heart that
he himself had been made sin, and nothing but sin.
And, indeed, in some ways, John came as near being
made sin as any mortal man ever came to that
unparalleled experience. John was the man of
sorrows till the true Man of Sorrows Himself
should come. All the appetites of John's body,
and all the affections of John's mind and heart,
were drunk up and drained dry by the all-consum-
ing fires of his unquenchable conscience. If all
sight and sense and conscience of sin had utterly
died out of Israel in that day, it had only died out
of all other men's hearts to rage like the bottomless
pit itself in the great broken heart of Elizabeth's
substituted son. And thus it was that the very
robbers ran and hid themselves among the rocks of
the hill-country when they saw that terrible man
standing again over against the city, and crying out,
"Oh Jerusalem! Jerusalem! how shalt thou abide
the day of His coming? For, behold! that day
shall burn as an oven. That great and terrible day,
when all that do wickedly shall be as the stubble!"
A man alone. A man apart. A great man. "A
greater man has never been born of woman," said He
who knew all men. "What went ye out into the
wilderness to see? A reed shaken with the wind!"
He who said that never smiled, say some. I see Him
smiling for once as He says that. 'A man clothed

in soft raiment! No; anything but that. And
anything but a reed; and with anything on but
the soft clothing that they put on in kings'
houses!'

And, now, from such a divinity-student as that,
and after thirty years of such a curriculum and
probationership as that, what kind of preaching
would you go to church to look for? A dumb dog
that cannot bark? A trencher-chaplain? A soft
thing of gown and bands and lawn sleeves? A
candidate for a manse and a stipend? "O generation of vipers, who hath warned you to flee from
the wrath to come? Bring forth, therefore, fruits
meet for repentance. And now the axe is laid at
the root of the trees. Therefore every tree
that bringeth not forth good fruit is hewn down
and cast into the fire. He that hath two coats
let him impart to him that hath none; and he
that hath meat, let him do likewise. Do violence
to no man. Neither accuse any man falsely, and
be content with your wages. He shall baptize you
with the Holy Ghost, and with fire. Whose fan is
in His hand, and He will gather the wheat into His
garner, but the chaff will He burn up with fire
unquenchable." The greatest preacher of the past
generation when preaching to a congregation of
young preachers said this to them: "He who has
before his mental eye the four last things will have
the true earnestness. He will have the horror and
the rapture of one who witnesses a conflagration, or
discerns some rich and sublime prospect above and
beyond this world. His countenance, his manner,

his voice will all speak for him in proportion as his
view has been vivid and minute.

> Yea, this man's brow, like to a title-leaf,
> Foretells the nature of a tragic volume.
> Thou tremblest, and the whiteness in thy cheek
> Is apter than thy tongue to tell thine errand.

It is this earnestness, in the supernatural order,
which is the eloquence of saints; and not of saints
only, but of all Christian preachers, according to the
measure of their faith and love."

But why, I wonder, was the forerunner able to
content himself all his days with being no more
than the forerunner? Why did John not leave off
his ministry of accusation and condemnation? Why
did he not wait upon, and himself take up, the
ministry of reconciliation? When he said to his
disciples, Behold the Lamb of God! why did the
Baptist not go himself with Andrew and the others
and become, first, a disciple, and then in due time
an apostle, of Jesus Christ? Zacharias's son would
have made a better son of thunder than both of
Zebedee's sons taken together. Why, then, did John
not leave the desert, and the Jordan, and follow
Christ? Well, to begin with, he could not help
himself. Jesus did not call John any more than He
called His own brother James. 'Go you,' John said
to Andrew, and to Peter, and to James and John, the
sons of Zebedee. 'Go you: I am not worthy to
enter under the same roof with Him. I will remain
where I am. I will work at the Jordan. I will
preach repentance, and He will teach you to preach

pardon. The Kingdom of Heaven is soon coming, but I shall not live to see it. I shall not live to see Tabor, and Calvary, and Olivet, and Pentecost, like you. He and you, His disciples, must increase, but I must decrease.' John was a great man and a great preacher, but, as we are wont to say, he never quite escaped out of the seventh of the Romans.

John the Baptist, like some much more evangelical men, was well-nigh smothered out of life in the slough of despond. 'Art thou He that should come, or do we look for another? Why dost thou eat and drink with Scribes and Pharisees, and leave me lying here in this prison-house of Herod and his harlots? Why dost thou eat and drink and make wine out of water for weddings? Rather, surely, should all God's true servants put on sackcloth and ashes and mourn apart, every family apart, and their wives apart. Art thou He that should come, or do we look for another?' Yes; this is Elias come back again. "I have been very zealous for the Lord," complained Elias in his cave in Horeb. "I only am left, and they seek my life. It is enough. Let me die, O Lord, for I am no better than my fathers." The God of all comfort be thanked for Elias, and for John, and for the slough of despond! They are all written for our rebuke, and for our learning, and for our sure consolation. Had these things not been written we would have turned away from our Bible in despair, saying: 'These men are giants and saints. These are not men of like passions as we are. Why,' we are often tempted to complain,

' Why is God's Kingdom so long in coming? What hinders it, if indeed Christ is on His throne and has all things in His hand? Why does He not burst open my prison-house and redress my cause? Why is my sanctification so postponed? Art thou He that should come, or do we look for another?' "Go and show John again those things that ye do see, and hear. The blind receive their sight, the lame walk, the lepers are cleansed, the deaf hear, the dead are raised up, and the poor have the Gospel preached to them. And blessed is he, whosoever shall not be offended in Me. He that believeth, and hopeth against hope, and endureth to the end, he alone shall be saved."

But by far the very best thing that the Baptist ever said or did was what he said to his jealous disciples · "A man can receive nothing," he said, " except it be given him from Heaven. He that hath the bride is the bridegroom. He must increase, but I must decrease." I would rather have had the grace from God to say that than have been the greatest man ever born of woman. For he who thinks, and says, and does a thing like that is born, not of blood, nor of the will of the flesh, nor of the will of man, but of God. And yet, when I come up close to it and look it in the face, this great utterance of the Baptist is not by any means so unapproachable as I took it to be at my first sight of it. I myself could have said and done all that John said and did that day. That is to say, had I been in his exact circumstances? For what were his exact circumstances? They were these, and much more than these. John

had drunk in the Sonship and the Messiahship of
Jesus of Nazareth with his mother's milk. And he
had been brought up all his days on that same
marrow of lions. His mother Elizabeth, you may
be very sure, did not die, nor did Zacharias depart
in peace, till they had both told over and over again
to their forerunner-son every syllable they had to
tell. And thus it was that for full thirty years John
did nothing else but wait for the Messiah. John
thought about no one else, and spake about no one
else, for all these endless years, but the Lamb of
God. And thus it was that when Jesus of Nazareth
came south to the Jordan to be baptized of John,
the Baptist remonstrated and refused, and said: "I
have need to be baptized of Thee." No, there was
nothing at all so great or so good in John's self-
effacing speech to his disciples. The most envious-
minded man in all the world does not envy a lion,
or an eagle, or an angel. A beggar does not envy
a king. He only envies his neighbour-beggar
whose pockets are so full of coppers and crumbs at
night. "Potter envies potter." And the more
theology there was in John's first great utterance,
"Behold the Lamb of God," the less morality
there was in his second great utterance, "He must
increase, but I must decrease." No thanks to John
not to be jealous of the Son of God! But had
Jesus been simply a carpenter of Nazareth, and
John's cousin to boot, turned suddenly such a
popular preacher with all men, and with all
John's baptized disciples going after him; and
had John, in that case, said all this about his

own decreasing, then I would down on the spot and kiss his feet.

"I was to preach in Clackmannan, where the most of the people were already for me to be their minister, but some that had the greatest power were against me, as it ordinarily fared with me in the places where I used to preach. On the Saturday afternoon there came a letter to my hand, desiring me to give the one-half of the day to another probationer, whom those who were against me had their eye upon. In these circumstances, seeing what hazard I was in of an evil eye, I committed the keeping of my heart to the Lord that I might be helped to carry evenly. He got the forenoon, for so it was desired by his friends. I was, as I expected, terribly assaulted by the tempter. When I came home from church my heart was in a manner enraged against itself on that account, and I confessed it before the Lord, abhorring myself, and appealing to God's omniscience, that I would fain have had it otherwise. As I was complaining that Satan had winnowed me, and had brought up much filthy stuff out of my heart, it came to my mind: 'But I have prayed for thee that thy faith fail not.' And then, in the evening, after service, while I sat musing over the day, I proposed this question to myself: Wouldest thou be satisfied with Christ as thy portion, though there was no hell to be saved from? And my soul answered, Yes! Supposing, further, wouldst thou be content with Christ, though likewise thou shouldest lose credit and reputation, and see other men before thee, and meet with much trouble and trial for His sake? And my soul answered, Yes! This was the last sermon I preached in Clackmannan, for I was going out of the country: and neither of us two preachers of that Sabbath was the person that God had designed for that pulpit."

He that hath the bride is the bridegroom.

LXXIV

NICODEMUS

THIS, I feel sure, is not the first time that Jesus of Nazareth and Nicodemus of Jerusalem have met. The sudden and trenchant way in which our Lord receives the cautious old ruler's diplomatic certificates and civilities, and every single word of the whole subsequent conversation, all point unmistakably, as I feel sure, to some previous meeting. The meeting took place in this wise; it must have taken place in some such wise as this:

Nicodemus was one of the oldest and most honoured heads of that overawing deputation which was sent out to Bethabara by the Temple authorities to examine into the Baptist's preaching, and to report to the Temple on that whole movement. "Who art thou?" Nicodemus demanded. "I am not the Christ," the Baptist answered. "Why baptizest thou then?" "I indeed baptize thee with water unto repentance, but, Behold the Lamb of God which taketh away the sin of the world, He will baptize thee, when thou comest to Him, with the Holy Ghost." And, had Nicodemus only been alone that day, there is no saying what he

might not have said and done on the spot.
Nicodemus was mightily impressed with all that
he had seen and heard at the Jordan. But he
was not free; he did not feel free and able to act
as his conscience told him he ought immediately to
act. He was at the head of that Temple embassy of
inquisition, and he simply could not extricate himself
from the duties, and the responsibilities, and the
entanglements of his office. He and his colleagues
had, by this time, seen and heard more than they
well knew what to say to the Temple about it all.
And, accordingly, glad to get away from Bethabara,
they took up their carriages and set out for Jerusalem, compiling all the way home their perplexing
and unsatisfactory report upon John and, especially
upon Jesus of Nazareth.

The third chapter of the Fourth Gospel is in many
things an absolutely classical chapter. In his third
chapter the fourth Evangelist introduces us into
an inquiry-room, as we would call it, in which our
Lord is the director and the counsellor of souls, and
in which Nicodemus is the inquirer and the convert.
Nicodemus had not slept soundly one single night,
nor spent one single day without remorse and fear,
ever since that scene when he saw Jesus of Nazareth
baptized by John, and coming up out of the water.
And thus it was that he stole out of the city that
night, and determined to see in secret this mysterious
man. I cannot put you back into Nicodemus's state
of mind as he stumbled out to Bethany in the dark
that night. To you, Jesus of Nazareth is the Son
of God, and your Saviour, and Lord, and Master.

But to Nicodemus that night Jesus of Nazareth
was—Nicodemus staggered and stood still—he was
afraid to let himself think Who and What Jesus of
Nazareth was, and might turn out to be. "Rabbi,
we know that thou art a teacher come from God."
But it took the old ruler's breath away when it was
answered him in such a sudden and sword-like way:
"Except a man be born of water and of the Spirit
he cannot enter into the Kingdom of God." To me
it is a most extraordinary and impossible hallucina-
tion. My whole mind and imagination and heart
and conscience would have to be taken down and
built up again upon an absolutely other pattern; my
whole experience, observation, and study of all these
divine things would have to be turned upside down
before I could possibly believe in what is called "bap-
tismal regeneration." No! there is no such thing.
Believe me, whoever says it, and however long
and learnedly and solemnly they have been saying it,
there is no such thing. There could not be. And,
certainly, there is no such materialistic, mechanical,
immoral, and unspiritual doctrine and precept
here. But there is in place of it a divine doctrine
and a divine precept that goes at one stroke down
into Nicodemus's self-deceiving heart, and cuts his
self-deceiving heart open to the daylight. If our
masters of Israel do not know what our Lord
pointed at when he said "water" with such em-
phasis, Nicodemus could have told them. And
had Nicodemus only been brave enough; had he
only had brow enough for a good cause; had he
only gone down into the waters of Jordan beside

Jesus of Nazareth, we would have been counting up to-day Peter, and James, and John, and Nicodemus, as all apostles of Christ. And we would have had an Epistle of Nicodemus to the Pharisees, and in it such a key to this whole conversation as would have made it impossible for any man to preach regeneration by water out of it. But Nicodemus missed his great opportunity, and both he and the whole Church of Christ have been terrible losers thereby down to this disunited and distracted day. Nicodemus, ruler of Israel just because he was, he was not equal to face such a loss of reputation and of other things as would immediately have descended upon him on the day he was publicly baptized. And as he lay and tossed on his bed every night after Bethabara, he thought he had at last devised a compromise so as to get into sufficient step with this teacher come from God, or whatever else He was, and yet not needlessly break with the Temple and its honours and emoluments. But there is no deceiving of Jesus Christ. For, have we not been told just before Nicodemus knocked at Martha's door, that Jesus knew all men, and knew what was in all men? And thus it was that Nicodemus had scarcely got his lips opened to pay his prepared compliments to our Lord when he was met again with that dreadful "water," which had haunted him like an accusing spirit ever since he had not gone down into it at Bethabara. Nicodemus stood ripe and ready for his regeneration, and for his first entrance into the kingdom of heaven, and he was within one short step of its gate at the Jordan, but that step was far too

strait and sore for Nicodemus to take. Nicodemus
saw the pearl, and knew something of the value of it,
but he could not make up his mind to sell all he
possessed so as to pay the price. In our Lord's
words, which He was always repeating, Nicodemus
had not the strength of mind and heart to take up
his cross and be born again. He was not able to
be baptized—not into regeneration, there is no such
baptism—but into evangelical repentance and the
open loss of all things. And thus it was that our
Lord, with all His affability, would not enter on any
closer intimacy or confidence with Nicodemus till
he had gone out to John at the Jordan. There
were a thousand things that held Nicodemus back
from John's baptism at his age and in his office, and
our Lord saw and sympathised with every one of
them. But, King of the kingdom of heaven as He
was that night in Bethany, even He could not
make the door of the kingdom one inch wider, or
one atom easier, than it was out at Bethabara.
'No!' our Lord said to Nicodemus, as he lay
struggling in the net of his old heart and life all
that night—'No! We do not need to talk any
more about my mighty works or your new birth.
You know your first duty in this whole matter
as well as I can tell you. John told you, and you
would not do it. And I cannot relieve you of
your first duty any more than I can do it for you.
And you may go away to-night, again leaving your
immediate duty undone, but mark my words, till
the day of your death and judgment there will
be no other way to a new heart and a new life for

you but to go out to the waters of Jordan and be
baptized of John before all Judea and Jerusalem,
and then come after Me and be My disciple.'
Nicodemus, that blind leader of the blind, had
always taken it for granted that when the kingdom
of God should come to Israel he would be taken
up to sit in one of the highest seats ot it. It had
never once entered his snow-white head to doubt
for one moment but that he would sit on a throne
up at the right hand of the Messiah. Imagine,
then, what a sudden blow in the face it was to
Nicodemus to be told, and that by the very Messiah
Himself, that he had neither part nor lot in that
kingdom, and could not have, until he had been
baptized in Jordan confessing his sins beside the
offscourings of the city.

At the same time, Nicodemus that night was in
Martha's house beside Jesus Christ, and not out at the
Jordan beside John the Baptist. And Jesus Christ
did not open the door and dismiss Nicodemus as
John the Baptist would certainly have done. The
very opposite. Our Lord, with His utmost tenderness for the ensnared and struggling old man, took
patience to put all John's best preaching over again
to Nicodemus, and added some of His own best
preaching to it, and, all the time, in His most
attractive and most winning way. John had scoffed
at Nicodemus's boasted birth from Abraham; but
Jesus contented Himself with simply saying that
Nicodemus must be born of water and of the Spirit.
John had assailed the Temple representatives as a
generation of vipers; and, while Jesus did not

withdraw or apologise for one single syllable of
His so-outspoken forerunner, He veiled His forerunner's strong language somewhat under the
sacramental and evangelical typology of the serpent in the wilderness.   And, then, from that
He went on to honour and to win Nicodemus
with that golden passage that "Even so must the
Son of Man be lifted up."   And that golden passage
was, I feel sure, Nicodemus's salvation that very
night, as it has been the salvation of so many sinners
ever since.   And then, as He shook hands with
Nicodemus just as the cock was crowing in Martha's
garden, Jesus said to Nicodemus, with a look and with
a manner that the old ruler never forgot, "But he
that doeth good cometh to the light, that his deeds
may be made manifest that they are wrought in
God."   John, our evangelist, was present all that
night, and he has written this chapter also of his
book so that we might believe that Jesus is the
Christ, the Son of God, and that believing we might
have life through His name.   And this evangelist,
after that ever-memorable day at Bethabara, and
that equally memorable midnight and morning at
Bethany, never lets Nicodemus out of his sight.
And thus it is that we read this in John's seventh
chapter: "Then Nicodemus said to the chief priests
and to the Pharisees, Doth our law judge any man
before it hear him, and know what he doeth?"
And then as we read John's nineteenth chapter,
we come on this. "And there came also Nicodemus,
which at the first came to Jesus by night, and he
brought a mixture of myrrh and aloes, about a
hundred pounds weight."

"And that golden passage was Nicodemus's salvation that very night, as it has been the salvation of so many ever since."

" Now I saw that there would be no answer to me till I had entire purity of conscience, and no longer regarded any iniquity whatsoever in my heart. I saw that there were some secret affections still left in me, which, though they were not very bad in themselves perhaps, yet in a life of prayer, such as I was then attempting, these remanent affections certainly spoiled all." Just so. Just so in Teresa, and in Nicodemus, and in you, and in me. It was surely not so very bad in itself for Nicodemus to let himself be put at the head of that Temple embassy of inquisition upon the Baptist. It was surely not so very bad in itself for Nicodemus, once having set out, to keep true to his colleagues, even if that was done somewhat at the expense and the injury of John. It was not such a great crime, surely, for Nicodemus to yield to such strong pressure so far as to put his name to the somewhat unfriendly report that his less scrupulous colleagues wrote out for the Temple. And it could only be good, surely, and to Nicodemus's credit, that he went out to Bethany at an hour most convenient for a ruler of the Jews. And it is not so very bad surely in itself in you—everybody does it—to take up a distaste at some man or some movement that you know quite well you have absolutely nothing against. It is surely not enough to cost you in the end the loss of your soul for you to think first of your prospects in life, and how you will continue to stand with this great man and with that, according as you cast in your lot with this party in the state, or with that denomination in the church.

Everybody does it. And who but John would denounce so fiercely and so contemptuously such secret affections as these are in you? But then, if John and then Jesus denounce, and despise, and deny you, what will it profit you if you gain the whole of this world? But, happily, there is a second lesson out of Nicodemus, and out of his subsequent history, and it is this: Though you have been a coward and a dark friend to truth and to duty up to this night, if God in His great goodness should give you yet another offer and opportunity, seize it on the spot. Jesus Christ is still among His enemies in many ways. Recognise and acknowledge Jesus Christ, and stand up for Him in your Sanhedrim like Nicodemus. Do you know Him? ask them. Have you ever gone to where He lodges and seen and heard Him for yourselves? Have you read the book you speak against? ask them. Do you love the writer, and do you wish him well? ask them. Do you rejoice in an evil report? demand boldly of them. Or do you rejoice, to your own loss, in the truth? The whole Seventy will turn on you, and will rend you. But what of that? For unless you are rent here for His name's sake, the Son of Man will be ashamed of you when He is suddenly revealed and suddenly descends on you in all His glory.

But for Nicodemus, and another timid friend to truth, the dead body of our Lord might have been taken out of the city and cast into the flames of Tophet, that type of Hell, along with the carcases of the two thieves. All the disciples had forsaken their crucified Master and had fled. But Joseph of Arimathæa and Nicodemus went boldly to Pilate and besought him to let them bury the dead body that all other men hid their faces from that day. And Joseph and Nicodemus took the body of Jesus and wound it in linen clothes with the spices, as the manner of the Jews is to bury their dead. It was the same Joseph of Arimathæa who had been a disciple of Jesus, but secretly for fear of the Jews; and it was the same Nicodemus, which at the first came to Jesus by night.

LXXV

PETER

THE Four Gospels are full of Peter After the name of our Lord Himself, no name comes up so often in the Four Gospels as Peter's name. No disciple speaks so often and so much as Peter. Our Lord speaks oftener to Peter than to any other of His disciples; sometimes in blame and sometimes in praise. No disciple is so pointedly reproved by our Lord as Peter, and no disciple ever ventures to reprove his Master but Peter. No other disciple ever so boldly confessed and outspokenly acknowledged and encouraged our Lord as Peter repeatedly did; and no one ever intruded, and interfered, and tempted Him as Peter repeatedly did also. His Master spoke words of approval, and praise, and even blessing to Peter the like of which He never spoke to any other man. And at the same time, and almost in the same breath, He said harder things to Peter than He ever said to any other of His twelve disciples, unless it was to Judas.

No disciple speaks so often as Peter. "Depart from me, for I am a sinful man, O Lord. Lo, we

have left all and followed Thee; what shall we have
therefore? Be it far from Thee, Lord; this shall
never be to Thee. Lord, if it be Thou, bid me
come unto Thee on the water. Lord, save me.
The crowd press Thee, and how sayest Thou, Who
touchéd me? Thou art the Christ, the Son of the
living God. To whom can we go but unto Thee?
Thou hast the words of eternal life. Lord, it is
good for us to be here; let us make three tabernacles:
one for Thee, and one for Moses, and one for Elias.
How oft shall my brother sin against me, and I
forgive him? Though all men deny Thee, yet will
not I. Thou shalt never wash my feet. Lord, not
my feet only, but also my hands and my head. I
know not the man. Lord, Thou knowest all things:
thou knowest that I love Thee." And, to crown all
his impertinent and indecent speeches, "Not so, Lord,
for I have never eaten anything that is common
or unclean." And then, in that charity which shall
cover the multitude of sins, "Forasmuch then as God
gave them the like gift as he did unto us; what
was I that I could withstand God?" These are
Peter's unmistakable footprints. Hasty, headlong,
speaking impertinently and unadvisedly, ready to
repent, ever wading into waters too deep for him,
and ever turning to his Master again like a little
child. Peter was grieved because He said unto him
the third time, Lovest thou me? And he said unto
Him, Lord, thou knowest all things: Thou knowest
that I love Thee.

The evangelical Churches of Christendom have no
duty and no interest to dispute with the Church of

Rome either as to Peter's primacy among the twelve
disciples, or as to his visits to Rome, or as to his
death by martyrdom in that city.   If the Church
of Rome is satisfied about the historical truth of
Peter's missionary work in the west, we are satisfied.
All that can be truthfully told us about Peter we
shall welcome.   We cannot be told too much about
Peter.   And as to his primacy that Rome makes so
much of, we cannot read our New Testament without coming on proofs on every page that Peter held
a foremost place among the twelve disciples.   In
that also we agree with our friends.   Four times the
list of elected men is given in the Gospels; and,
while the order of the twelve names varies in all
other respects, Peter's name is invariably the first in
all the lists, as Judas's name is as invariably the last.
The difference is this: The New Testament recognises
a certain precedency in Peter, whereas the Church
of Rome claims for him an absolute supremacy.   The
truth is this.   The precedency and the supremacy
that Peter holds in the Four Gospels was not so
much appointed him by his Master; what supremacy
he held was conferred upon him by nature herself.
Peter was born a supreme man.   Nature herself, as
we call her, had, with her ever-bountiful and original
hands, stamped his supremacy upon Peter before he
was born.   And when he came to be a disciple of
Jesus Christ he entered on, and continued to hold,
that natural and aboriginal supremacy over all in-
ferior men, till a still more superior and supreme
man arose and took Peter's supremacy away from
him.   We all have the same supremacy that Peter

had when we are placed alongside of men who are
less gifted in intellect, and in will, and in character,
than we are gifted.   Peter's gifts of mind, and force
of character, and warmth of heart, and generosity of
utterance—all these things gave Peter the foremost
place in the Apostolic Church till Paul arose.   But
Peter, remarkable and outstanding man as he was,
had neither the natural ability nor the educational
advantages of Saul of Tarsus.   His mind was neither
so deep nor so strong nor so many-sided nor at all
so fine and so fruitful as was Paul's incomparable
mind.   And as a consequence he was never able to
come within sight of the work that Paul alone could
do.   But, at the same time, and till Paul arose and all
but totally eclipsed all the disciples who had been
in Christ before him, Peter stood at the head of
the apostolate, and so leaves a deeper footprint on
the pages of the Four Gospels at any rate, than any
of the other eleven disciples.

John was intuitive, meditative, mystical.   Philip
was phlegmatic, perhaps.   Thomas would appear to
have been melancholy and morose.   While Peter was
sanguine and enthusiastic and extreme both for
good and for evil, beyond them all.   Peter was
naturally and constitutionally of the enthusiastic
temperament, and his conversion and call to the
discipleship did not decompose or at all suppress his
true nature; the primal elements of his character
remained, and the original balance and the proportion of those elements remained.   The son of Jonas
was, to begin with, a man of the strongest, the most
wilful, and the most wayward impulses; impulses

that, but for the watchfulness and the prayerfulness
of his Master, might easily have become the most
headlong and destructive passions. "Christ gives
him a little touch," says Thomas Goodwin, "of some
wildness and youthfulness that had been in Peter's
spirit before Christ had to do with him. When
thou wast young thou girdedst thyself and walkedst
whither thou wouldest. But when thou art old,
thou shalt stretch forth thy hands, and another
shall gird thee, and carry thee whither thou wouldest
not. Peter had had his vagaries, and had lived
as he liked, and, Peter, says Christ to him, when
thou art hung up by the heels upon a cross, there
to be bound to thy good behaviour, see that thou,
remembering what thou wast when young, show
them thy valour and thy resolution when thou
comest to that conflict; and Peter remembered it,
and was moved by it.—2 Peter i. 14." Such, then,
was Peter's so perilous temperament, which he had
inherited from his father Jonas. But by degrees,
and under the teaching, the example, and the
training of his Master, Peter's too-hot heart was
gradually brought under control till it became the
seat in Peter's bosom of a deep, pure, deathless love
and adoration for Jesus Christ. Amid all Peter's
stumbles and falls this always brought him right
again and set him on his feet again—his absolutely
enthusiastic love and adoration for his Master.
This, indeed, after his Master's singular grace to
Peter, was always the redeeming and restraining
principle in Peter's wayward and wilful life. To
the very end of his three years with his Master,

Peter was full of a most immature character and an unreduced and unbridled mind and heart. He had the making of a very noble man in him, but he was not easily made, and his making cost both him and his Master dear. At the same time, blame Peter as much as you like; dwell upon the faults of his temperament, and the defects of his character, and the scandals of his conduct, as much as you like; I defy you to deny that, with it all, he was not a very attractive and a very lovable man. "The worst disease of the human heart is cold." Well, with all his faults, and he was full of them, a cold heart was not one of them. All Peter's faults, indeed, lay in the heat of his heart. He was too hot-hearted, too impulsive, too enthusiastic. His hot heart was always in his mouth, and he spoke it all out many a time when he should have held his peace. So many faults had Peter, and so patent and on the surface did they lie, that you might very easily take a too hasty and a too superficial estimate of Peter's real depth and strength and value. And if Peter was for too long like the sand rather than like the rock his Master had so nobly named him, the sand will one day settle into rock, and into rock of a quality and a quantity to build a temple with. If Peter is now too forward to speak, he will in the end be as forward to suffer. The time will come when Peter will act up to all his outspoken ardours and high enthusiasms. In so early designating the son of Jonas a rock, his Master was but antedating some of Simon's coming and most characteristic graces. His Divine Master saw in Simon latent qualities of

courage, and fidelity, and endurance, and evangelical humility that never as yet had fully unfolded
themselves amid the untoward influences round about
his life.   In any case, an absolute master may surely
name his own servant by any name that pleases him;
especially a Royal Master; for the Sovereign in every
kingdom is the true fountain of honour.   Whatever, then, may be the true and full explanation,
suffice it to us to know that our Lord thus saluted
Simon, and said to him, Simon, son of Jonas, thou
shalt be called Cephas, which is, by interpretation,
a rock.

Of the four outstanding temperaments then,
Peter's temperament was of the ardent and enthusiastic order.   And, indeed, a deep-springing,
strong - flowing, divinely - purified, and divinely-
directed enthusiasm is always the best temperament
for the foundation and the support of the truly prophetic, apostolic, and evangelic character.   For what
is enthusiasm?   What is it but the heart, and the
imagination, and the whole man, body and soul, set
on fire?   And the election, the call, the experience,
and the promised reward of the true prophet, apostle,
and evangelist, are surely enough to set on fire and
keep on fire a heart of stone.   It was one of the
prophetic notes of the coming Messiah's own temperament that the zeal of God's house would eat
Him up.   And there is no surer sign that the same
mind that was found in Jesus Christ is taking possession of one of His disciples than that he more
and more manifests a keen, kindling, enthusiastic
temper toward whatsoever persons and causes are

honest, and just, and pure, and lovely, and of good report; just as there is nothing more unlike the mind and heart of Jesus Christ than the mind and heart of a man who cares for none of these things. Let us take Peter, come to perfection, for our pattern and our prelate; and, especially, let us watch, and work, and pray against a cold heart, a chilling temper, a distant, selfish, indifferent mind.

Closely connected with Peter's peculiar temperament, and, indeed, a kind of compensation for being so possessed by it, was his exquisite sense of sin. We see Peter's singular sensitiveness and tenderness of spirit in this respect coming out in a most impressive and memorable way on the occasion of his call to the discipleship. Andrew was not an impenitent man. John was not a hard-hearted man. But though they both saw and shared in the miraculous draught of fishes on the sea of Galilee, Peter alone remembered his sins, and broke down under them, in the presence of the power and grace of Christ. "Depart from me, O Lord, for I am a sinful man." "No; fear not," said his Master to Peter, "for from henceforth thou shalt so catch men." Peter's prostrating penitence at such a moment marked Peter out as the true captain of that fishing fleet that was so soon to set sail under the colours of the Cross to catch the souls of men for salvation. That sudden and complete prostration before Christ at that moment seated Peter in a supremacy and in a prelacy that has never been taken from him. And there is no surer sign of an evangelically penitent and a truly spiritual man than this — that his prosperity in life always calls back to him his past sins and his abiding ill-desert. He is not a novice in the spiritual life to whom prosperity is as much a means of grace as adversity. They are wise merchantmen who make gain in every gale; who are enriched in their souls not only in times of trial and loss, but are still more softened and sanctified amid all their gains and all their comforts both of outward and inward estate. Well may those mariners praise the Lord for His goodness whose ships come home sinking with the merchandise they have made in the deep waters. But still more when, with all their prosperity, they have the broken heart to say, He hath not dealt with us after our sins, nor rewarded us according to our iniquities.

It was Peter's deep and rich temperament, all but completely sanctified, that made Peter so forgetful of himself as a preacher, and so superior to all men's judgments, and so happy, to use his own noble words, to be reproached for the name of Christ. Can you imagine, have you come through any experience that enables you to imagine, what Peter's thoughts would be as he mounted the pulpit stairs to preach Judas's funeral sermon? Judas had betrayed his Master. Yes. But Peter himself; Peter the preacher; had denied his Master with oaths and curses. And yet, there is Peter in the pulpit, while Judas lies a cast-out suicide in Aceldama! 'O the depths of the Divine mercy to me! That I who sinned with Judas; that I who had made my bed in hell beside Judas; should be held in this honour, and should be ministering to the holy brethren! O

to grace how great a debtor!' And again, just
think what all must have been in Peter's mind as he
stood up in Solomon's porch to preach the Pentecost
sermon. That terrible sermon in which he charged
the rulers and the people of Jerusalem with the
dreadful crime of denying the Holy One and the
Just in the presence of Pilate. While he, the
preacher, had done the very same thing before a few
serving men and serving women. You may be sure
that it was as much to himself as to the murderers
of the Prince of Life that Peter went on that day to
preach and say, " Repent, therefore, that your sins
may be blotted out ; since God hath sent His Son
to bless you, in turning away every one of you from
his iniquities." The truth is, by this time, the
unspeakably awful sinfulness of Peter's own sin had
completely drunk up all the human shame of it. If
they who know about Peter's sin choose to reproach
him for it, let them do it. It is now a small matter
to Peter to be judged of men's judgment. They
sang David's Psalms in Solomon's porch ; and that
day Peter and the penitent people must surely have
sung and said, " Wash me thoroughly from mine
iniquity, and cleanse me from my sin. For I
acknowledge my transgression, and my sin is ever
before me. Restore to me the joy of thy salvation,
and uphold me with thy free spirit. Then will I
teach transgressors thy ways, and sinners shall be
converted unto thee." And if preachers pronounced
benedictions after their sermons in those days, then
we surely have Peter's Solomon's-porch benediction
preserved to us in these apostolic words of his: " Ye

therefore, beloved, seeing ye know all these things, beware lest ye also fall from your steadfastness. But grow in grace, and in the knowledge of our Lord and Saviour Jesus Christ, to whom be glory both now and for ever. Amen."

LXXVI

JOHN

JOHN, fisherman's son and all, was born with one of the finest minds that have ever been bestowed by God's goodness upon any of the sons of men. We sometimes call John the Christian Plato. Now when we say that our meaning is that John had by nature an extraordinarily rich and deep and lofty and beautiful mind. John had a profoundly intuitive mind. An inward, meditating, brooding, imaginative, mystical, spiritual mind. Plato had all that, even more perhaps than John. But, then, Plato had not John's privileges and opportunities. Plato had not been brought up on the Old Testament, and he had only had Socrates for his master. And thus it is that he has only been able to leave to us the *Symposium*, and the *Apology*, and the *Phœdo*. Whereas John has left to us his Gospel, and his Epistles, and his Apocalypse. John has the immortal honour of having conceived and meditated and indited the most magnificent passage that has ever been written with pen and ink. The first fourteen verses of John's Gospel stand alone

E

and supreme over all other literature, sacred and
profane. THE WORD WAS GOD, AND THE WORD
WAS MADE FLESH. These two sentences out of John
contain far more philosophy; far more grace, and
truth, and beauty, and love; than all the rest that
has ever been written by pen of man, or spoken by
tongue of man or angel. Philo also has whole
volumes about the Logos. But the Logos in Philo,
in Newman's words, is but a "notion": a noble
notion, indeed, but still a cold, a bare, and an
inoperative notion. Whereas the WORD of John
is a Divine Person; and, moreover, a Divine Person
in human nature: a revelation, an experience, and
a possession, of which John himself is the living
witness and the infallible proof. I have heard of
him by the hearing of the ear, said Philo. But
mine eyes have seen and mine hands have handled
the Word of Life, declares John. And, with the
WORD MADE FLESH, and set before such eyes as
John's eyes were, no wonder that we have such
books from his hands as the Fourth Gospel, the
First Epistle, and the Apocalypse.

How did John sink so deep into the unsearchable
things of his Master, while all the other disciples
stood all their discipleship days on the surface?
What was it in John that lifted him so high above
Peter, and Thomas, and Philip, and made him first
such a disciple, and then such an apostle, of wisdom
and of love? For one thing it was his gift and
grace of meditation. John listened as none of
them listened to all that his Master said, both in
conversation, and in debate, and in discourse. John

thought and thought continually on what he saw
and heard. The seed fell into good ground. John
was one of those happy men, and a prince among
them, who have a deep root in themselves. And
the good seed sprung up in him an hundredfold.
The first Psalm was all fulfilled in John. For he
meditated day and night on his Master, and on
his Master's words, till he was like David's tree that
was planted by the rivers of water so that its leaf
never withered, nor was its fruit ever wanting in its
season. Meditate on Divine things, my brethren.
Be men of mind, and be sure you be men of meditation. Mind is the highest thing, and meditation is
the highest use of mind; it is the true root, and
sap, and fatness of all faith and prayer and spiritual
obedience. Why are our minds so blighted and so
barren in the things of God? Why have we so
little faith? Why have we so little hold of the
reality and nobility of Divine things? The reason
is plain—we seldom or never meditate. We read
our New Testament, on occasion, and we hear it
read, but we do not take time to meditate. We
pray sometimes, or we pretend to pray; but do we
ever set ourselves to prepare our hearts for the
mercy-seat by strenuous meditation on who and
what we are; on who and what He is to whom
we pretend to pray; and on what it is we are to
say, and do, and ask, and receive? We may never
have heard of Philo, but we all belong to his barren
school. The Lord Jesus Christ is but a name and
a notion to us; a sacred name and notion, it may be,
but still only a name and a notion. The thought

of Jesus Christ seldom or never quickens, or over-
awes, or gladdens our heart. Whereas, when we
once become men of meditation, Jesus Christ, and
the whole New Testament concerning Him, and the
whole New Jerusalem where He is preparing a place
for us, will become more to us than our nearest
friend: more to us than this city with all its most
pressing affairs. Our conventional morning chapter
about what Jesus Christ did and said, and is at
this moment doing and saying, will then be far more
real to us than all our morning papers and all our
business letters. Nor is this the peculiar opportunity and privilege of men of learning only. John
was not a man of learning. John was described as
an ignorant and an unlearned man, though all the
time he was carrying about in his mind the whole
of the Fourth Gospel. My brethren, meditate on
John's Gospel. Meditate on that which was not
made without long, and deep, and divinely-assisted
meditation. You may be the most unlearned man
in this learned city to-night, and yet such is John's
Gospel, and such is the power and the blessedness
of meditation on it, that John will look down on
you after your house is asleep to-night, and will say
over you, as you now sit, and now stand, and now
kneel with his Gospel in your hands—" That which
we have seen and heard declare we unto you, that
you may have fellowship with us; and truly our
fellowship is with the Father and with His Son
Jesus Christ."

Meditation with imagination. All that John
writes is touched and informed and exalted with this

divinest of all the talents. The Apocalypse, with all its splendours, was in God's mind toward us when He said, Let us make Zebedee's son, and let us make him full of eyes within. Do not be afraid at the word "imagination," my brethren. It has been sadly ill-used, both name and thing. But it is a noble name and a noble thing. There is nothing so noble in all that is within us. Our outward eye is the noblest of all our outward organs, and our inward eye is the noblest of all our inward organs. And its noblest use is to be filled full of Jesus Christ, as John's inward eye was. John did not write his Apocalypse without that great gift in its fullest exercise. And we cannot read aright what he has written without that same exercise. We cannot pray aright without it. We cannot have either faith or love aright without it. And just in the measure we have imagination, and know how to use it, we shall have one of the noblest instruments in our own hand for the enriching and perfecting of our whole intellectual and spiritual life. I do not say that the Book of Revelation is the noblest product of John's noble imagination. For, all that was within John, imagination and meditation and love, was all moved of the Holy Ghost up to its highest and its best in the production of the great Prologue to the Fourth Gospel. At the same time, it is in the Revelation that John's glorified imagination spreads out its most golden wings and waves them in the light of heaven. Only it will take both meditation and imagination to see that. But to see that will be one of our best lessons from this greatly-gifted and greatly-blessed apostle to-night.

And, then, as was sure to come to pass, the disciple of meditation and imagination becomes at last the apostle of love. At the Last Supper, and as soon as Judas had gone out, Jesus said to the eleven, " A new commandment I give unto you, that ye love one another. As I have loved you, that ye also love one another. By this shall all men know that ye are my disciples, if ye have love one to another." Eleven thoughtful and loving hearts heard that new commandment and the comfort that accompanied it. But in no other heart did that Divine seed fall into such good ground as in his heart who at that moment lay on Jesus' bosom. "Little children, love one another," was the aged apostle's whole benediction as the young men carried him into the church of Ephesus every Lord's Day. And when he was asked why he always said that, and never said any more than that, he always replied, " Because this is our Lord's sole commandment, and if we all fulfil this, nothing more is needed. For love is the fulfilling of the law."

LXXVII

MATTHEW

MATTHEW loved money. Matthew, like Judas, must have money. With clean hands if he could; but, clean hands or unclean, Matthew must have money. Now, the surest way and the shortest way for Matthew to make money in the Galilee of that day was to take sides with Cæsar and to become one of Cæsar's tax-gatherers. This, to be sure, would be for Matthew to sell himself to the service of the oppressors of his people; but Matthew made up his mind and determined to do it. Matthew will set his face like a flint for a few years and then he will retire from his toll-booth to spend his rich old age in peace and quietness. He will furnish a country-house for himself up among the hills of Galilee, and he will devote his last days to deeds of devotion and charity. And thus it was that Matthew, a son of Abraham, was found in the unpatriotic and ostracised position of a publican in Capernaum. The publicans were hard-hearted, extortionate, and utterly demoralised men. Their peculiar employment either already found them all that, or else it soon made them all that. " Publicans

and sinners " ; "publicans and harlots"—we continually come on language like that in the pages of the
four Gospels.   Well, Matthew had now for a long
time been a publican in Capernaum, and he was fast
becoming a rich man.   But, over against that, he had
to content himself with a publican's companionships,
and with a publican's inevitable evil conscience.
Matthew could not help grinding the faces of the
poor.   He could not help squeezing the last drop
of blood out of this and that helpless debtor.   His
business would not let Matthew stop to think who
was a widow, and who was an orphan, and who
was being cruelly treated.   The debt was due, it was
too long overdue, and it must be paid, if both the
debtor and his children have to be sold in the
slave-market to pay the debt.

   Jesus of Nazareth, the carpenter's son, knew
Matthew the publican quite well.   Perhaps, only
too well.   Jesus and His mother had by this time
migrated from Nazareth to Capernaum.   He had
often been in Matthew's toll-booth with His mother's
taxes, and with other poor people's taxes.   Even if
not for Himself and for his widowed mother, the
carpenter would often leave His bench to go to
Matthew's toll-booth to expostulate with him, and
to negotiate with him, and to become surety to him
for this and that poor neighbour of His who had
fallen into sickness, and into a debt that he was not
able to pay.   The sweat of Jesus' own brow had
oftener than once gone to settle Matthew's extortionate charges.   ' If he hath wronged thee, or oweth
thee aught, put that to mine account.   I, Jesus, the

son of Joseph, have written it with mine own hand, I
will repay it '—that would stand in Matthew's books
over and over again, till Matthew was almost ready
to sell the surety Himself.   But by this time Jesus,
first of Nazareth and now of Capernaum, who had
been every poor widow's cautioner for her rent and
for her taxes, had left His father's inherited workshop, and had been baptized by John into a still
larger Suretyship.   And thus it is that He is back
again in Capernaum, no longer a hard-working carpenter, mortgaging all His week's wages and more
for all His poor neighbours.   But he is now the
Messiah Himself!   And Matthew in his toll-booth
has a thousand thoughts about all that, till he cannot
get his columns to come right all he can count.   And
till one day, just as He was passing Matthew's well-
worn doorstep, a widow woman of the city, with her
child in her arms, rushed up against our Lord, and
exclaimed to Him : "Avenge me of mine adversary!"
till she could not tell Him her heart-breaking tale
for sobs and tears.   And then, with that never-to-
be-forgotten look and accent of mingled anger and
mercy, our Lord went immediately into the publican's
office and said to him : 'Matthew, thou must leave
all this life of thine and come and follow Me.'
Matthew had always tried to stand well out of eye-
shot of our Lord when He was preaching.   He felt
sure that the Preacher was not well disposed toward him, and his conscience would continually say
to his face, How could He be?   But at that so
commanding gesture, and at those so commanding
words, the chains of a lifetime of cruelty and extor-

tion fell on the floor of the receipt of custom; till, scarcely taking time to clasp up his books and to lock up his presses, Matthew the publican of Capernaum rose up and followed our Lord.

Matthew does not say so himself, but Luke is careful to tell us that Matthew made a great feast that very night, and gathered into it a supper-party of his former friends and acquaintances that they might see with their own eyes the Master that he is henceforth to confess, and to follow, and to obey. What a sight to our eyes, far more than to theirs, is Matthew's supper-table to-night! There sits the publican himself at the head of the table, and the erewhile carpenter of Capernaum in the seat of honour beside him. And then the whole house is full of what we may quite correctly describe as a company of social and religious outcasts. An outcast with us usually means some one who has impoverished, and demoralised, and debauched himself with indolence and with vice till he is both penniless in purse and reprobate in character. We have few, if any, rich outcasts in our city and society. But the outcast publicans of that night were well-to-do, if not absolutely wealthy men. They were men who had made themselves rich, and had at the same time made themselves outcasts, by siding with the oppressors of their people and by exacting of the people more than was their due. And they were, as a consequence, excommunicated from the Church, and ostracised from all patriotic and social and family life. What, then, must the more thoughtful of them have felt as they entered Matthew's

supper-room that night and sat down at the same
table with a very prophet, and some said—Matthew
himself had said it in his letter of invitation—more
than a prophet. And, then, all through the supper,
if He was a prophet He was so unlike a prophet;
and, especially, so unlike the last of the prophets.
He was so affable, so humble, so kind, so gentle,
with absolutely nothing at all in His words or in
His manner to upbraid any of them, or in any way
to make any of them in anything uneasy. They
had all supped with Matthew before, but that was
the first night for many years that any man with
any good name to lose had broken bread at the
publican's table. He had given suppers on occasion
before, but Jesus had never been invited, nor Peter,
nor James, nor John. And it was the presence of
Jesus and His disciples that night that led to the
scene which so shines on this page of the New Testament. For there were Pharisees in Capernaum in
those days, just as there were publicans and sinners.
And just as the publicans were ever on the outlook
for more money; and just as the sinners were ever
on the outlook for another supper and another
dance; so the Pharisees were ever on the outlook
for a fresh scandal, and for something to find fault
with in their neighbours. "Why eateth your
Master with publicans and sinners?" the Pharisees
of Capernaum demanded of Jesus' disciples. And
the disciples were still too much Pharisees themselves to be able to give a very easy answer to that
question. But Jesus had his answer ready. Grace
was poured into His lips at that opportune moment

till He replied: "They that be whole need not a
physician, but they that are sick. I came not to
call the righteous, but sinners to repentance." Long
years afterwards, when Matthew was writing this
autobiographic passage in his Gospel, the whole
scene of that supper-party rose up before him like
yesternight. 'Jesus, now in glory,' he said to himself, 'was sitting here, as it were. James and John
there. Myself at the door, divided between wel-
coming my old companions and warning them off.
Some Pharisees from the synagogue are coming up
with their lamps. Then their loud and angry
voices; and then His voice with more pity in it
than anger, calling sinners to repentance.' It was a
night to be remembered by Matthew.

When Matthew rose up and left all and followed
our Lord, the only thing he took with him out of
his old occupation was his pen and ink. And it is
well for us that he did take that pen and ink
with him, since he took it with him to such
good purpose. For, never once did our Lord sit
down on a mountain side or on a sea-shore to teach
His disciples; never once did He enter a synagogue
and take up the Prophets or the Psalmists to preach;
never once did He talk at any length by the
way, that Matthew was not instantly at His side.
Till Matthew came to be known not so much as
Matthew the disciple, or as the former publican of
Capernaum, but rather as that silent man with the
sleepless pen and ink-horn. It needed a practised,
and an assiduous, and an understanding pen to take
down the Sermon on the Mount, and to report and

arrange the parables, and to seize with such correctness and with such insight the terrible sermons of his Master's last week of preaching. But Matthew did all that, and we have all that to this day in his Gospel. The bag would have been safe, and it would have been kept well filled, in Matthew's money-managing hands, but Matthew had far more important matters than the most sacred money matters to attend to. What a service, above all price, were Matthew's hands ordained to do as soon as his hands were washed from sin and uncleanness in the Fountain opened in that day! What a service it was to build that golden bridge by which so many of his kinsmen according to the flesh at once passed over into the better covenant, the Surety of which covenant is Christ! "The Gospel according to St. Matthew: the Book of the generation of Jesus Christ, the son of David, the son of Abraham." "Saintliness not forfeited by the penitent," is the title of one of our finest English sermons, and, it may here be added, neither is service.

"And Matthew the *publican*." Now, we would never have known that but for Matthew himself. Neither Mark, nor Luke, nor John, nor Paul ever calls Matthew by that bad name. It is Matthew himself alone who in as many words says to us, "Come, all ye that fear God, and I will tell what He has done for my soul." It is Matthew himself alone who publishes and perpetuates to all time his own infamy. Ashamed of himself, both as a publican and an apostle, till he cannot look up, the text is the only footprint of himself that St. Matthew leaves behind him on the sands of Scripture. Our first Gospel is his holy workmanship, and this text, so deeply imbedded into it, is the sure seal of its author's Christian temper and Apostolic character. "Position and epithet are indicative both of natural humility and modesty, as well as of evangelical self-abasement."

"They that be whole need not a physician, but they that are sick." Happy intrusion, and fortunate fault-finding of the Pharisees which ended in these ever-blessed words of our Saviour! And then, these words also: "I am not come to call the righteous, but sinners to repentance." Sick and sinful men, do you hear that? Are you truly and sincerely sick with sin? Then He who has made you sick will keep you sick till you come to Him to heal you. Are you a sinner with an evil life holding you like a chain in a cruel, an unclean, a hopeless bondage? Then—

> He comes! the prisoners to relieve,
>   In Satan's bondage held;
> The gates of brass before Him burst,
>   The iron fetters yield.
>
> He comes! from darkening scales of vice
>   To clear the inward sight;
> And on the eyeballs of the blind
>   To pour celestial light.
>
> He comes! the broken hearts to bind,
>   The bleeding souls to cure:
> And with the treasures of His grace
>   T' enrich the humble poor.

Are you that prisoner? Are you held in Satan's bondage? Is your inward sight clogged up with the scales of vice? Is your heart broken? And is your very soul within you bleeding? Are you a publican? Are you a sinner? Are you a harlot? Look at Matthew with his Gospel in his hand! Look at Zacchæus restoring fourfold! Look at Mary Magdalene, first at the sepulchre. Look unto Me, their Saviour says to thee also: Look unto Me, and be thou saved also. And so I will!

> Thy promise is my only plea,
> With this I venture nigh:
> Thou callest burden'd souls to Thee,
> And such, O Lord, am I.

LXXVIII

ZACCHÆUS

THERE was a soft spot still left in Zacchæus's heart, and that soft spot was this: Zacchæus was as eager as any schoolboy in all Jericho to see Jesus who He was. And like any schoolboy he ran before and climbed up into a sycamore tree to see Jesus, for He was to pass that way. And simple things like that, childlike and schoolboy-like things like that, always touched our Lord's heart. Of such is the kingdom of Heaven, He was wont to say when He saw simplicity like that, and self-forgetfulness, and naturalness, and impulsiveness, or anything else that was truly childlike. We would not have done what Zacchæus did. We are too stiff. We are too formal. We have too much starch in our souls. Our souls are made of starch, just as Bishop Andrewes's soul was made of sin. But starch is more deadly than sin. Your soul may be saved from sin, but scarcely from starch. "Curiosity and simplicity," says Calvin, "are a sort of preparation for faith. Nay, it was not without a certain inspiration from heaven that Zacchæus climbed up into that sycamore tree. There was

a certain seed of true piety in his heart when he
so ran before the press, and so climbed up into that
sycamore tree," so says on this subject the greatest
of all the commentators upon it.

Had our Lord considered public opinion He
would have looked straight before Him when He
came to that sycamore tree, and would not have let
His eyes lift till He was well past Zacchæus's perch.
But our Lord was as simple and as natural and
as spontaneous that day as Zacchæus was himself.
Our Lord paid no attention to the prejudices or to
the ill-will of the populace. The more ground
there was for their prejudices and their ill-will the
more reason there was to Him why He should stop
under Zacchæus's tree and call him to come down.
The windows and the walls and the roofs of Jericho
were all loaded with sightseers that day, but our
Lord did not stop under any of them. It was at
Zacchæus's sycamore tree alone that our Lord stopped
and looked up and said : " Zacchæus, make haste and
come down, for to-day I must abide at thy house."
All Zacchæus's past life, all his real blamefulness,
all the people's just and unjust prejudices, and all
the bad odour of Zacchæus's class, it all did not for
one moment turn our Lord away from Zacchæus's
house. Had our Lord asked Himself—What will
the people think and say, He would not have im-
perilled His popularity in Jericho by sitting at the
tax-gatherer's table. But one of our Lord's absolute
rules of life and conduct was to make Himself at all
times and in all places of no reputation. And thus
it was that the thought of how Jericho would take

F

it never for one moment entered our Lord's mind.
Not for years had any man who wished to stand
well with the people so much as crossed Zacchæus's
threshold. Zacchæus, with all his riches, was a
very lonely man. He was a well-hated and a uni-
versally-avoided man. And thus it was that our
Lord's conduct that day towards him completely
overcame Zacchæus. He could not believe his own
eyes and ears. That this great Prophet, whose face
he had been so breathless to see, should actually
stop and call his name, and invite Himself to his
house, and that He should actually be walking with
him back to his house! Zacchæus was well-nigh
beside himself with amazement and with delight.
That halt under the sycamore tree, that summons
of our Lord, that walk back together through the
astonished and angry streets, and then the supper
and the conversation over it and after it—all that
entered into and at last completed Zacchæus's
salvation. Are you a minister, or an elder, or a
missionary, or a district visitor? Then, sometimes,
invite yourself to the hospitality of the poor, and
the outcast, and the sunken, and the forlorn.
Knock civilly at their door. Ask the favour of a
chair and a cup of cold water. Join them in their
last crust. And see if salvation does not from that
day begin to come to that house also.

I cannot get it out of my mind the deep share
that Matthew the publican must have had in the
conversion of Zacchæus. You remember all about
Matthew. How he was sitting in his toll-booth
one day when Jesus came up to him and said:

"Follow me." And how Matthew left all and followed Him. And how Matthew made Him a great feast, and how the scribes and Pharisees found fault, and said to the disciples, Why do ye eat and drink with publicans and sinners? And especially, you can never forget our Lord's golden answer: "They that are whole need not a physician, but they that are sick." Well, do you not think that Matthew must have had an intense interest in Zacchæus that night? Even if the eleven supped and lodged elsewhere in the city that night, our Lord would be sure to take Matthew with Him in order to encourage and to advise Zacchæus. When two members of any craft come together you know how they draw to one another and forget the presence of all the rest, there is such a freemasonry and brotherhood between them. They have so many stories to tell, experiences to compare, confessions to make, and confidences to share, that those who are not of the same occupation know nothing about. It is now going on to three years that Matthew has been a disciple, but it is like yesterday to him to look back to his receipt of custom. And when Jesus suddenly stopped under the sycamore tree that day and said, Zacchæus, come down, and when Zacchæus dropped that moment at our Lord's feet, no one's heart in all the crowd went out to the trembling little tax-gatherer like Matthew's heart. And all that night the two publicans had scarcely broken ground on all they had to tell one another. ' If He calls you to leave all and follow Him, you must do it at once. You will never repent it. You have no idea of

Him. What a man He is, and what a master; and, how it is all to end, God only knows. But if He invites you to join us. I beseech you not to hesitate for one moment.' 'Tell me all about yourself,' said Zacchæus. 'What did He say to you? And how did you manage to cut off, and leave for ever behind you, the work and the wealth of your whole life so soon and so completely?' And Matthew told Zacchæus all we know, and far more that we need not listen to, for we would not understand it. Till, what Zacchæus stood forth and said next morning before our Lord, and before all Jericho, was fully as much at Matthew's instance and dictation as at Zacchæus's own repentance and resolution. 'Behold, Lord, I have made up my mind overnight, and I wish you and all men to know it—the half of my goods I give to the poor; and if I have taken anything from any man by false accusation, I restore him fourfold.' Brave little gentleman! By that noble speech of thine thou hast added more than many cubits to thy stature! Thy bodily presence, say they, is weak, and thy height contemptible; but all thine after life will be weighty and powerful!

"It is a determined rule in divinity," says a great divine, "that our sins can never be pardoned till we have restored that which we unjustly took away, or which we wrongfully detain. And this doctrine, besides its evident and apparent reasonableness, is derived from the express words of Scripture, which reckons restitution to be a part of repentance, and necessary to the remission of sins. For these are the determined words of Scripture—If the wicked restore the pledge, and give again that he hath robbed, and walk in the statutes of life, without committing inquity, he shall surely live; he shall not die. None of his sins that he hath committed shall be mentioned unto him; he hath done that which is lawful and right, he shall surely live."

LXXIX

LAZARUS

AZARUS of Bethany comes as near to
Jesus of Nazareth, both in his character, and in his services, and in his
unparalleled experiences, as mortal
man can ever come. Lazarus's name
is never to be read in the New Testament till the
appointed time comes when he is to fall sick, and to
die, and to be raised from the dead, for the glory of
God. Nor is his voice ever heard. Lazarus loved
silence. He sought obscurity. He liked to be over-
looked. He revelled in neglect. You could have
taken any liberty you pleased with Lazarus with
the most perfect impunity. Our Lord and His
twelve disciples often found where to lay their head
in Martha's house, as it was called. But where
Lazarus laid his head at such times no one ever asked.
The very evangelists pass over Lazarus as if he were
a worm and no man. They do not give him the
place of a man in his own house. But Lazarus never
takes offence at that. 'He is a sheep,' said the men and
the women of Bethany. And so he was. For, when
Jesus of Nazareth and His twelve disciples came to
Martha's house, Lazarus hewed wood, fetched water,

and washed the feet of the whole discipleship; and then, when they were all asleep, 'though he was the staff and sustentation of the family,' he supped out of sight on the fragments that remained. All Bethany was quite right, Lazarus was a perfect sheep. They laughed him to scorn, they shot out the lip at him, and he never saw it. At any rate, he never returned it. Let Martha sweat and scold; let Mary sit still and listen; and let Lazarus only be of some use to them, that he would never believe he was, and that was Lazarus's meat and drink. So much so, that the world would never have heard so much as Lazarus's name unless the glory of God had been bound up with Lazarus's sickness, and death, and resurrection.

Our Lord had this happiness, that He loved all men whether they loved Him or no. But there were some men that He loved with a quite special and peculiar love. And Lazarus was one of the most eminent of those men. But, even in our Lord's love to His friend, Lazarus is pushed back almost out of sight. Martha and Mary always come in before their brother in our Lord's love, as in everything else. This evangelist, that bare record according as he saw, had seen his Master's love to Martha and Mary many a time; but it was only now and then that he had the opportunity of seeing either Lazarus's love to his Lord, or his Lord's love to Lazarus. Lazarus loved his Lord far more than they all. But his love had this defect about it that it was a silent love. It was what we call a worshipping love. It was a wholly hidden love. Only, Lazarus's love could not elude His eyes Who knows what is in man without man testifying what is in him. And He so loved Lazarus back again, and so expected all His disciples to love Lazarus also, that He was wont to call Lazarus their universal friend. "Our friend Lazarus sleepeth," He said. For Lazarus by that time, for the glory of God, and for the glory of the Son of God, had fallen into a fatal sickness. And Martha had despatched a swift messenger to Bethabara beyond Jordan to summon Him and to say, Lord, he whom Thou lovest is sick. 'Trouble not the Master,' Lazarus had said to his sister in his sickness. 'The Jews of late sought to stone Him, and wouldest thou bring Him hither again?' And with a great shame and a great pain at himself for so troubling his sister and his Master, and with a great hunger in his heart for his Father's house in heaven, Lazarus turned his face to the wall and fell asleep.

Lazarus is altogether left out by us as we read this heavenly chapter. We leave out Lazarus in glory even more completely than he was left out by all men in this life. We leave out of this chapter heaven itself also as much as if we were all Sadducees. And not till we have our eyes opened to the ascended Lazarus, and to his throne in glory, will we ever read this magnificent chapter aright, or at all aright understand why in all the world Jesus should groan and weep all the way to where Lazarus's dead body lay and decayed in the grave. Our Lord did not leave Lazarus out. No, nor his glory either. Our Lord knew what He was on His way to do, and He took to heart what He was on His way to do, and it repented Him to a groaning that could not be uttered, to work His last miracle for the awakening of Jerusalem at such a cost to Lazarus. He knew all the time how it would all end. He knew what Caiaphas would say. And He knew what Judas and Pilate and Herod and the people would do. And He groaned in His spirit because He so clearly foresaw that His friend Lazarus, like Himself, was to be such a savour of death in them that perish, and at such a price to Lazarus.

> So o'er the bed where Lazarus slept,
> He to His Father groan'd and wept:
> What saw He mournful in that grave,
> Knowing Himself so strong to save?
>
> The deaf may hear the Saviour's voice,
> The fetter'd tongue its chain may break:
> But the deaf heart, the dumb by choice,
> The laggard soul that will not wake,
> The guilt that scorns to be forgiven :—
> These baffle e'en the spells of Heaven:
> In thought of these, His brows benign,
> Not even in healing cloudless shine.

Jesus wept. Yes: and if you saw a friend of yours in glory, and then saw also that he was to be summoned to lay aside his glory and to return to be a savour of death to so many of your fellow-citizens, you could not but weep also. Even if you knew that it was the will of God, and for the glory of the Son of God, your friend was coming, you could not but weep. And our Lord wept because Lazarus, who had been but four days in glory, was to be summoned to lay aside his glory

and to return to this world of sin and death, and
that on such an errand; an errand, as it would
issue, of exasperation and final hardness of heart
to his enemies. Chrysologus, the Chrysostom of
Ravenna, has it: " When our Lord was told of
Lazarus's death He was glad; but when He came
to raise him to life, He wept. For, though His
disciples gained by it, and though Martha and
Mary gained by it, yet Lazarus himself lost by it,
by being re-imprisoned, re-committed, and re-sub-
mitted to the manifold incommodities of this life."

" This last and greatest of His miracles was to
raise our Lord much estimation," says the distinguished John Donne, " but (for they always
accompany one another) it was to raise both Him
and Lazarus much envy also." And I will always
believe that the sight of Lazarus's share in this
terrible tragedy mingled with the sight of His own
share. Dante wept when he saw that he had to
return to envious Florence from the charity of
Paradise, even though it was to compose *The Commedia* for God and for the world. And Teresa has
it that Lazarus entreated his Master not to summon him back to this life for any cause whatsoever.
But it was to be to Lazarus as it was to be to
his Master, and that is enough. " Now is my soul
troubled: and what shall I say ? Father, save me
from this hour; but for this cause came I unto this
hour. Father, glorify Thy name."

And thus it was that scarcely had Lazarus sat
down in his Father's house: he had not got his
harp of gold well into his hand: he had not got

"*This last and greatest of His miracles was to raise our Lord much estimation, but (for they always accompany one another) it was to raise both Him and Lazarus much envy also.*"

the Hallelujah that they were preparing against
the Ascension of their Lord well into his mouth,
when the angel Gabriel came up to where he sat,
all rapture through and through, and said to
him: 'Hail! Lazarus: highly honoured among the
glorified from among men. Thy Master calls up
for thee. He has some service for thee still to do
for Him on the earth.' And the sound of many
waters fell silent for a season as they saw one of the
most shining of their number rise up, and lay aside
his glory, and hang his harp on the wall, and pass
out of their sight, and descend to where their
heavenly Prince still tarried with His work unfinished. And Lazarus's soul descended straightway
into that grave, where for four days his former
body had lain dead, and towards which our Lord
was now on His way. And the first words that
Lazarus heard were these, and the voice that spake
was the voice of his former Friend—"Father, I thank
Thee that Thou hast heard me. And I knew that
Thou hearest me always. Lazarus, come forth."
And he that was dead came forth bound hand and
foot with grave clothes; and his face was bound
about with a napkin. And Jesus wept at the con-
trast between heaven and earth, and said, "Loose
him, and let him go." Just where did Lazarus go?
Like himself, he no doubt hid himself till his Master
would not eat till Lazarus was called. For they
made our Lord a supper again in those days, and
Martha served again, and Lazarus this time was
one of them that sat at the table with Him. But
the chief priests consulted that they might put

Lazarus also to death: because that by reason of him many of the Jews went away and believed on Jesus.

Whether they carried out their counsel and put Lazarus to death the second time we are not told. The evangelist to whom we owe Lazarus had not room within his limits to tell us any more about Lazarus. But a post-canonical author has these entries in his Arabic diary, which I will faithfully copy out for your satisfaction about Lazarus. The entries are abrupt, and unfinished, and broken off, and sometimes quite unintelligible, as you will see. 'The man had something strange and unearthly in the look of him.' ' He eyed the world like a child.' ' He was obedient as a sheep, and innocent as a lamb.' 'He let them talk.' ' A word, a gesture, a glance from a child at play, or in school, or even in its sleep, would startle him into an agony.' ' His heart and brain moved there, his feet stay here.' ' Often his soul springs up into his face.' 'The special marking of the man is prone submission to the will of God.' ' He merely looked with his large eyes on me.' ' He loves both old and young; able and weak; he affects the very brutes, and birds, and flowers of the field.' 'The man is harmless as a lamb, and only impatient at ignorance and sin.' You can construct for yourselves out of these authentic fragments what Lazarus's second life was as long as the chief priests let him alone.

God's great demands that He sometimes makes on His great saints, is the great lesson that Lazarus teaches us. As, also, that great lowliness of mind.

and great meekness, and great self-surrender, is our
greatest saintliness. And, accordingly, that God
made His greatest demands on His own lowly-
minded Son, the meekest and the most self-emptied
of all men. And, after Him, on Lazarus the friend
of His Son. A demand on Lazarus that made his
divine Friend mourn and weep for him, as he came
down to earth to comply with the demand. Lazarus
was the most lamb-like of men in all the New Testament, next to the Lamb Himself; and his services
and his experiences were, if after a long interval,
yet not at all unlike the services and the self-
surrenders and the self-emptyings of his Master.
For Lazarus also laid aside his glory.

Now, God's work in this world demands this very
same meekness, and lowly-mindedness, and self-empti-
ness, and laying aside of our own glory, from some
men among us every day. And God's work stands
still in our hands, and all around us, just because He
has no men like-minded with Jesus of Nazareth and
Lazarus of Bethany. Who will offer themselves to
take up the kenotic succession? Some humiliation,
some self-emptying, some surrender, as of heaven
itself in exchange for earth, may be demanded of
you as your contribution to the glory of God, and
to the glory of the Son of God. Something that
will make your best friends groan and weep for you,
as Lazarus's best friend groaned and wept for him.
Yes; God may have as terrible a service to ask of
you, when you are ready for it, as when He asked
His own Son to go down to Bethlehem, and to
Nazareth, and to Gethsemane, and to Calvary.

Some self-emptying and self-sacrifice like that He asked of the glorified Lazarus also, when He sent him back to Bethany which was so nigh unto Jerusalem. Are you able? Are you ready? Are you willing to be made able and ready? Let your answer be the answer of Jesus of Nazareth, and of Lazarus of Bethany: "Lo, I come. In the volume of the book it is written of me, I delight to do Thy will, O my God; yea, Thy law is within my heart."

LXXX

THE WOMAN WITH THE ISSUE
OF BLOOD

UR Lord was on His way to raise the ruler's little daughter from the dead. Now, this woman who overtook Him on the way was not actually dead like the ruler's little daughter, but she often wished she was, for she was worse than dead. She had tried everything for her deadly disease. There was not a physician far nor near that she had not consulted as to whether he could cure her. She had spent all her living upon physicians, till, to-day, she is beside herself with downright despair. And so am I. I am not dead, but I often wish I were. For I, too, am all my life sick to death. And I have tried everything. Every preacher, every author, every discipline, every medicine of the soul. And I am worse to-night than ever I was. I am in a strait betwixt two. I love my work more than ever. I love my family more than ever. No man ever loved his family more than Martin Luther did, but all the time he told his hearers who had head enough and heart enough to understand him, that he had no real joy

in his children because of his sin.   And I, for one,
am exactly like Luther in that.

But to return to the text.   "And a certain
woman, which had an issue of blood twelve years,
and had suffered many things of many physicians,
and had spent all that she had, and was nothing
bettered but rather worse — when she heard of
Jesus, came in the press behind, and touched the
hem of His garment.   For she said within herself,
If I may but touch His clothes I shall be whole.
And straightway the fountain of her blood was
dried up, and she felt in her body that she was
healed of her plague."   Well, blood is blood; and
blood is bad enough; but blood at its worst is not
sin.   Sin is SIN.   Sin has no fellow.   Sin has no second,
unless it is death and hell.   Sin tries Christ Himself
to His utmost, as this woman's bloody issue tried
and found wanting all the best physicians in all the
cities round about.   Christ could cure a twelve year
old issue of blood incidentally, and just by the way,
as we say ; ere ever He was aware He had healed that
woman of her blood, but not for all her remaining life
of her sin.   All her days, you may depend upon it,
she was nothing better of her sin, but rather worse.
None of the three evangelists tell it, but it is as true
as if they had all told it in the same words.   She
followed Him about with her sin wherever He went.
She went up to Jerusalem after Him with her sin.
She was one of the women who were beholding
afar off when He died on the tree for her sin.   She
often went out all her days to the Garden of
Gethsemane, and lay all night on her face because

of her sin. And sometimes at a passover season, and such like, she felt in herself as if she was going to be healed this time ; but, before the sun set, she was worse with her secret sinfulness than ever. And, till her innermost soul ran pure sin day and night, and would not be staunched of heaven or earth. And all that is our own very exact case to a scriptural parable. Long after we have sold all to win Christ ; long after He has begun at times to shed abroad all that He has promised to shed abroad in our heart; long after that we will still be nothing better, but infinitely far worse. One stolen touch was sufficient for an issue of blood; but a long and close lifetime of absolute clasp of Christ will not heal us of our sin. Oh, the malice of sin ! Oh, the height, and the depth, and the hold, and the absolute incurableness, of sin ! Only, with all that we must not despair. We must not go back. We must not give over. Even if it is incurable, let us not say so. It is ; but let us not say it even within ourselves. Let us be like this bleeding woman. To-night, put out your hand and touch Christ. Never mind the gaping crowd pressing behind and before on Him and on you. They are nothing to you, and you are nobody to them. Never mind what they do, or do not do. They are not bleeding to death like you, and they are no rule to you. They did not come up here to-night on your errand. You are as good as dead, and this may be your last chance of Christ. Make a grasp at Him. Make a great grasp, however unceremonious and desperate, at the hem of His garment. Actually

G

stretch out your hand where you now sit, and the stretch of your hand will sacramentally help your heart. Never mind the people in the same seat staring at you, and thinking you are mad. So you are, and you need not sit and look as if you were not. Never mind that you have not all your days till to-night so much as once touched Christ by faith. This woman had suffered enough to drive her beside herself for twelve years before she ever thought of the hem of His garment, and she went home that night healed of her plague. Press through, and grasp tight, and hold fast till you hear Him say, 'Somebody is detaining me.' And till you go home laughing in your guilty heart at your new-found peace and strength and joy. What a power you have, O sinner, and what an opportunity! "Somebody hath touched Me; for I perceive that virtue has gone out of Me."

And then, if you succeed in touching Him to-night, you must not do that once for all, and never again. You must touch Him every day; and if you will not call me extravagant, and carried away, I will say—Do the same thing every hour and every moment of the week. One thing all the week is needful. And that is to keep that hem firm in your hand. Even when you feel completely dis-enchanted of this scripture and this night and this house; even when you feel shame as you look back at your intensity to-night; even when you feel that this woman, and Christ, and this church, and the present preacher are all a piece of the same entire dream—still grope after His garment. Believe in

Him and in His garment. Keep believing and keep praying when no one knows. Lift up your heart to Him even in the press of business, and among the cumber of the house, and week-day and all. And He will let down into your hand the hem of His High Priestly garment, all tingling with bells, and all laden with pomegranates, and all shining with strength and with beauty. And when again your evil heart runs with envy, and anger, and pride, and ill-will, and unkindness, and all the rest of the bad blood of hell,—all that the more grasp you at Him and at His garment. It is like the precious ointment upon the head, that ran down upon the beard, even Aaron's beard, that went down to the skirts of his garment: His grace and His salvation, that is. Here love runs down, and here joy in your neighbour's joy, and here sweetness of temper, and here humility of mind, and here goodwill, and here attraction to people, and here brotherly kindness, and all the rest of that holy oil.

> The healing of His seamless dress
>   Is by our beds of pain ;
> We touch Him in life's throng and press,
>   And we are whole again.

Now, why was it, did you ever think, that when our Lord healed so thoroughly this woman's sick body, He did not in an equally immediate, and in an equally thorough way, heal her far more sick soul? Why did He stop short at her blood? Why did He not work a far better cure on her sin? Was it because she was not sick of sin? Was it because she

had not come, with all those twelve years, to know
the plague of her own heart? Or was it because
He did not come the first time to this world with a
full salvation? Or was it, and is it, because sin is
such a mystery of iniquity that it takes not only
both His first and His second comings to heal our
souls of sin; but long time, and great labour, and
great pain, and great faith, and great prayer on our
part also, before even His Divine power can perform
and pronounce a perfect cure? Yes, that is it. Be
sure that it is. Even if this woman had come on a
very much better errand than she did come; and
with a far better kind of faith and love; even had
she come as David and Paul and Luther came all
their days; she would only have gone home to a
more horrible pit in her own heart than ever, and
to a more corrupt and abominable and burdensome
body of death than ever, and to a loneliness that
the happiest home in Canaan could not have com-
forted; to a lifelong death indeed, of which her
twelve years' issue of blood was but a far off and
feeble emblem. Did you ever read Richard Baxter's
Reasons why the Rest that remains for the people
of God is never entered on and enjoyed here?
What a splendid debate that seraphic preacher holds
with all those saints of God whose hearts are broken
continually with an unalleviable pain and with an
insatiable hunger after holiness. What depths, both
in God and man, Baxter sounds on that great
subject, and what heights he scales! O my brethren,
be pleaded with to read almost exclusively the books
that are pertinent to your sinful and immortal souls

—such as *The Saint's Rest*. Listen to the great saints as they come together to tell and to hear from one another what God has done for their souls. And O, as many of you as are torn to pieces every day with the torture of sin, as well as covered with inward shame at the degradation and pollution of sin, keep yourselves in life by hope. You are saved by hope. Keep every day numbering your days, and forecasting that Great Day on which Christ shall come to you and shall make you perfect as He and His Father are perfect. Give reins to your imagination and think,—all sin for ever gone! Think of that! All sin gone clean out of your sinful heart for ever! I cannot believe it possible. All things are possible to me but that. I, for one, will not be the same man, if ever that crowning work of Omnipotence is wrought in me. I will not know myself, that it is myself. Now, nothing but sin and misery; and then, nothing but love, and holiness, and unspeakable blessedness. This horrible and loathsome incubus, myself, for ever cast off, and for ever cast down into the depths of hell, never to come up again. And I set free from myself for ever, and admitted to the New Jerusalem to walk with Christ and with His saints, in all the holiness and all the beauty of the Divine Nature! "Comfort ye, comfort ye my people, saith your God. Speak ye comfortably to Jerusalem, and cry to her that her warfare is accomplished, that her iniquity is pardoned. What are these which are arrayed in white robes? and whence came they? These are they which came out of great tribulation. And

God shall wipe all tears from their eyes. And
there shall be no more death, neither sorrow, nor
crying, neither shall there be any more pain: for
the former things are passed away. And He that
sat upon the throne said to me: These things are
true and faithful."

LXXXI

MARY MAGDALENE

THERE is a still unsettled dispute among New Testament scholars as to how many Marys there are in the Gospels, and then as to their identification. But our dispute will not be as to this Mary or that, but only as to ourselves. No, nor even as to who and what were the seven devils that at one time had made such a hell in Mary Magdalene's heart. Our whole dispute and debate shall be to let in some light from heaven on the bottomless pit of our own hearts, so as to scare out of our hearts some of the seven devils who still haunt and harbour there.

> Seven times
> The letter that denotes the inward stain,
> He on my forehead, with the truthful point
> Of his drawn sword inscribed. And, 'Look,' he cried,
> When enter'd, that thou wash these scars away.'

We do not know just what Mary Magdalene's seven scars were. But for our learning, Dante's own seven scars are written all over his superb autobiographical book. And Dante's identical scars are inscribed again every returning Fourth Day in

Bishop Andrewes's *Private Devotions*. Solomon
has the same scars also: "These six things doth the
Lord hate. Yea, seven are an abomination unto
Him." And, again: "When he speaketh fair,
believe him not, for there are seven abominations in
his heart." And John Bunyan has the very same
number at the end of his *Grace Abounding*: "I find
to this day these seven abominations in my heart."
And then Bunyan is bold enough, and humble-
minded enough, to actually name his scars for the
comfort and encouragement of his spiritual children.
Now, what are your seven scars? What are your
seven abominations in your heart? What are the
six things, yea seven, in your heart that the Lord
hates? It is almost our whole salvation to ask and
to answer that question. Because it is a law of
devils; it is their diabolical nature, and it is a first
principle of their existence and indwelling and possession of a man, that they never make their presence
known in any man till he begins to name them and
curse them and cast them out. He does not at all
feel their full power, and the whole pain, and shame,
and distress, and disgust of their presence till he is
almost delivered from them. They rage and roar
and tear and gnash our hearts to pieces when they
begin to see that their time in us is to be short.
But, till then, we are absolutely insensible to their
very existence, either outside of us or inside. It
was an old aphorism of the deep old divines, and
they took it, if I mistake not, out of the deep old
stoics: "All vices are in all men; but all vices are
not all extant in all men." As much as to say:

'All the seven devils are in every man's heart, but they do not all rage and rend equally in every man's heart: no, nor in the same man's heart at all times. The very devils have their times and their seasons like everything else.' Now, though Mary Magdalene is my text, it is of little real interest or importance to me who and what her seven devils were, unless in so far as that would cast some light in upon my own possession; yours and mine. But, on the other hand, if I have come by any means to know something of the terrible plague of my own heart, then, in that measure, I am a real authority as to the Marys of the four Gospels; and especially as to Mary Magdalene. To have grappled long, even with one inward devil, and to have had him at my throat day and night for years, and I at his— that is true New Testament scholarship. That throws a flood of light on all the Marys who followed our Lord about, and that makes Mary Magdalene a minister's own and peculiar field, and his specialised department of pulpit work. And the same inward experience is making not a few of my hearers far better genealogists, and harmonists, and exegetes, and demonologists, than all their teachers.

Pride, envy, anger, intemperance, lasciviousness, covetousness, spiritual sloth—these were Dante's seven scars on his sanctified forehead. I had a great dispute on the subject of Dante's scars the other day with one of the best Dante scholars in this country. He contended against me with great learning and great eloquence that Dante's besetting

sin was pride—a towering, satanic, scornful pride,
to the contemptuous and complete exclusion of all
possible envy. He had Dante on his side in one
passage at any rate. I could not deny that. And
I confess it seemed to me that Dante and he
together had established the doctrine that any
envy at all is absolutely, and in the nature of things,
quite incompatible with such a lofty pride as that
was which wholly possessed Dante's heart. Till,
staggered, if not truly convinced, I gave in: so
browbeaten was I between two such antagonists.
But when I came to myself; when I left all books,
the very best, about pride and envy, and when I
was led again of God's Holy Spirit into the pandemonium that is in my own heart, I recovered
courage, till, to-night, I have my harness on again
to fight the battle of divine truth against any man,
and all men, and even Dante himself. And the
divine truth to me in this matter is this: That
in my heart, if not in Dante's, both pride and envy
have their full scope together; and that they never,
in the very least, either exclude, or drink up, or
narrow down, the dreadful dominion of one another.
Now, what do you say to that? How is it with
your heart? 'I have no books,' said Jacob
Behmen. 'I have neither Aristotle, nor Dante,
nor Butler, nor Brea, nor Shepard, nor Edwards;
I have only my own heart.' You have none of
these books either, but you surely have your own
heart. Who, then, for the love of the truth, will
so read his own heart as to take sides with me?
Come away. Take courage. Speak out. Speak

boldly out. You must surely know what pride is, and you must all know, still better perhaps, what envy is, and at whose payments and praises and successes and positions your heart cramps and strangles and excruciates itself. Do you not both know and confess all these things before yourself and before God every day? Do you not? O stone-dead soul! O sport and prey of Satan! O maker of God a liar, and the truth is not in you! I would not have your devil-possessed heart, and your conscience seared with a redhot iron, for the whole world. I would rather be myself yet, and myself at my worst, a thousand times, than be you at your best. Whether you are true enough and bold enough to be on my side or no, I shall not be so easily silenced in my next debate about these two devils. For a man is more to himself, on such inward matters, than the whole *Commedia* and the whole *Ethics* to boot, with all their splendid treasures of truth, and power, and experience, and eloquence. As I was saying, I have not the least notion as to who or what Mary Magdalene's seven devils were, and much less do I know how they could possibly be all cast out of her heart in this life. I do not know much, as you will see, about Mary Magdalene, but I would not give up the little knowledge I have of myself, no, not for the whole world. For what would it profit me if I gained the whole world of knowledge and everything else, and lost my fast-passing opportunity of having all this pandemonium that is within me for ever cast out of me?

I will confess it again: How the whole seven could possibly be cast out of her heart in this present life, I, for one, cannot imagine; and I do not believe it. Complete, or all but complete, deliverance from two, say, of the seven I could easily believe, but the remaining five are quite beyond me. Two of the seven scars are on the surface. They are but skin-deep. Two of Dante's seven devils have their holes in the sand; in the soft earth and on the exposed outside of our hearts. Properly speaking, they are rather mole-heaps and rabbit-burrows than the dens of devils. Properly speaking, they are not devils at all. Till any man who is in any earnest at all can easily dig them out with a spade, and wring their necks, and nail their dead carcases up on the church door and be for ever done with them. But if you do that with those two it will only the more terrify and exasperate the other five. When the outposts of hell are stormed and taken and put to the sword, that only drives the real hell, with its true and proper devils, deeper down into their bottomless entrenchments. There are some wild beasts so devilish in their bite; they make their cruel teeth so to meet and lock fast in a man's flesh; that the piece has to be cut out if he is to be saved from their deadly hold. And the fangs of these five genuine devils must be broken to pieces in their heads with the hammer of God, and the flesh and bone into which they have locked their cursed teeth must be cut out and sacrificed before the soul is set free. And in this case the surgeon with his hammer and his knife is Death, and the full science

and success of his operations will not be all seen till
the Resurrection morning. "Like as a lion that is
greedy of his prey, and as it were a young lion
lurking in secret places. Arise, O Lord ! disappoint
him, cast him down. As for me, I will behold
Thy face in righteousness ; I shall be satisfied, when
I awake, with Thy likeness." It is better to enter
into heaven with seven devils excavated out of our
hearts as with a knife, than to have them gnawing
in our hearts to all eternity.

Since ever there were women's hearts in this
world, were there ever two women's hearts with
such emotions in them as when Mary the mother of
Jesus, and Mary Magdalene, stood together beside
His Cross? Did you ever try to put yourself into
His mother's heart that day, or into Mary Magdalene's heart? They stood and wept as never another
two women have wept since women wept in this
world, till John at Jesus' command took His mother
away from Calvary and led her into the city. But
Mary Magdalene still stood by the Cross. He dismissed His mother, but He kept Mary ; she would
not be dismissed, and she stood near to His crucified
feet. All His disciples had forsaken Him and fled.
And thus it was that there was no eye-witness left
to tell us how Mary Magdalene stood close up to
the Cross weeping, and how she did wash His feet
with her tears, and did wipe them with the hairs
of her head. And then, when He said, I thirst,
how she took the sponge out of the soldier's hand
and put it up to His lips. When He bowed His
head she saw Him do it, and she heard Him say, It

is finished! It was not a place for a woman. But
Mary Magdalene was not a woman; she was an
angel. She was the angel who strengthened Him.
She was the whole Church of God and ransomed
bride of Christ at that moment in herself: she and
her twin-brother, the thief on the Cross. How the
next three days and three nights passed with Mary
Magdalene I cannot account for her to you. But
on the first day of the new week cometh Mary
Magdalene early, when it was yet dark, unto the
sepulchre. And Jesus saith unto her, Mary! She
turned herself, and saith unto Him, Rabboni! Jesus
saith to her, 'Touch me not with thy tears, nor
with the hairs of thy head, nor with thy ointment.'
And, had He not said that, she would have been
holding His feet there to this day. And now that
He has ascended to His Father's house, He is saying
to His saints and to His angels to this very day the
very same words that He said in Simon's house—
"This woman since I came in hath not ceased to kiss
my feet."

But the supreme lesson to me out of all Mary
Magdalene's marvellous history is just the text:
"He appeared first to Mary Magdalene, out of
whom He had cast seven devils." As much as to
say,—it was not to Peter, nor to James, nor to
John, that He gave that signal favour and unparalleled honour. It was not even to His own
mother. It was to Mary Magdalene. It was to
her who loved Him best, and had the best reason to
love Him best, of all the men and women then living
in the world. While this world lasts, and as long

as there are great sinners and great penitents to comfort in it, let Mary Magdalene be often preached
upon, and let this lesson be always taught out of
her, this lesson,—that no depth of sin, and no possession of devils even, shall separate us from the love
of Christ. That repentance and love will outlive
and overcome everything; as also, that there is no
honour too high, and no communion too close, for
the love of Christ on His side, and for the soul's love
on her side, between them to enjoy. Onlyrepentdeep
enough and to tears enough; only love as Mary
Magdalene loved Him who had cast her seven devils
out of her heart; and He will appear to you also,
and will call you by your name. And He will employ you in His service even more and even better
than He honoured and employed Mary Magdalene
on the morning of His Resurrection.

Mary Magdalene! my sister, my forerunner into
heaven till I come, and my representative there!
But, remember, only till I come. Cease not to kiss
His feet till I come, but give up thy place to me
when I come. For to whom little is forgiven, the
same loveth little. Give place then; give place to
me before His feet!

LXXXII

THE MOTHER OF ZEBEDEE'S CHILDREN

WHY does the Evangelist write the text in that round-about way? Why does he not write the text in his own simple and straightforward style? Why does he not simply say: Salome, the mother of James and John? I do not know for certain why the Evangelist writes in that ambiguous and intentionally obscure way, but I will tell you what I think about it. By the time that Matthew sat down to compose his Gospel, James, the eldest son of Zebedee and Salome, had already been a long time in heaven with Christ; and John, his brother, was a high and an honoured Apostle in the Church of Christ on earth. James had long ago drunk of Christ's cup and been baptized with Christ's baptism. While John was, by this time, as good as the author of the Fourth Gospel, and the three Epistles, and the Apocalypse. All the same, nay, all the more, John had not forgotten the sins and the faults and the follies of his youth; and, above all, he had not forgotten that for ever disgraceful day when he got his mother to beg the best throne for him and for his brother. That disgraceful day though now so long past was ever before John. And thus it was, as I think, that Matthew wrote in this roundabout way about it. 'May my right hand forget its cunning,' said Matthew, 'before I bring back a single blush to that great saint of God! No enemy of Christ and of His Church shall ever blaspheme out of my book if I can help it.' And thus it was that this Evangelist took a garment, and laid it on his shoulder, and went backward, till he had all but completely covered up the sin of Salome and James and John. 'Blessed Antonomasiast!' exclaimed John, when he read this chapter of Matthew for the first time. 'Yes,' said John; 'all Scripture is indeed given by inspiration of the Spirit of God: and God is love!' And it was so certainly with this special Scripture. For Matthew's heart of love and honour for John had taken his inspired pen out of his hand at the opening of this passage till this stroke of sheltering style was struck out before the writer knew what he is doing. Dante is full on every page of his of this same exquisite device. Dante, indeed, is the fullest of this exquisite device of any of the great writers, either sacred or profane. But the Bible had this exquisite device, as it had all Dante's exquisite devices, long before he was born. And still the Bible is by far our finest education in morals, and in manners, and in love, and in letters, as well as in our everlasting salvation.

'Leave it to me, my sons,' said Salome; 'leave it to me. Do not be in any doubt about it. It will all come right. I am not to be His mother's sister for nothing, and I have not followed Him about all

H

this time, and ministered to Him out of my substance, for nothing. Blood is thicker than water,'
she said, 'and you, my sons, will see that it is so.
Leave it to me. Who is Andrew? And who is
Peter? And who is their father? And who is their
mother, I would like to know, that they should
presume to be princes over my sons? It shall never
be! Leave it to me, my sons; leave it to me.'
"Then came to Him the mother of Zebedee's children with her sons, worshipping Him, and desiring
a certain thing of Him. And He said to her, What
wilt thou? She saith unto Him, Grant that my two
sons may sit, the one on Thy right hand and the
other on the left, in Thy Kingdom." Well done,
Salome! Well done! As long as this Gospel is
preached this splendid impudence of thine shall be
told of thee! 'Let the sons of all the other mothers
in Israel sit, or stand, or lie as they like; only, let
my two sons sit high above them all, and have their
feet on the necks of all the ten.' Had Salome's
presumption been less magnificent, our Lord would
have been very angry at her. But the absolute
sublimity of her selfishness completely overcame
Him. He had met with nothing like it. The
splendid humility of the Syrophœnician woman
completely overcame Him, and now He is equally
overcome with the splendid shamelessness of Salome's
request. Her cold-blooded cruelty to Himself also
pierced His heart as with a spear. This is the
Monday, and He is to be betrayed on the Thursday,
and crucified on the Friday. All the same, Salome
went on plotting and counter-plotting for a throne

for her two sons that only existed in her own stupid and selfish heart. And it was the sight of all this that made our Lord's rising anger turn to an infinite pity, till He said to her two sons: 'Are ye able to drink of My cup, and to be baptized with My baptism?' And what do you think the two insane men said? They actually said: "We are able!" In such sin had their mother Salome conceived them. In such stupidity of mind. In such hopeless selfishness, combined with such hard-hearted presumptuousness. And then, that it should be John! That it should be the disciple who had been chosen to such a coming sanctification and to such a coming service! That it should be John, who had been so loved, and so trusted, and so leaned upon, and so looked to! And at this time of day, that John should be so deep in this miserable plot. Our Lord often spoke about a daily cross. Well, that was His cross that Monday, and a very bitter cross it was. More bitter to His heart by far than all the thorns and nails and spears of next Friday. What a cup of red wine that miserable mother and her two sons like her, made our Lord to drink that day! 'O Salome,' He said, 'and O James and John her sons, you little know the baptism you are all baptizing Me with. But your own baptism, also, will soon come. And mine is at the door.'

A little imagination, with a little heart added to it, would have saved Salome and her two sons from making this shameful petition. Salome should have said to herself something like this. She should have said this, and should have dwelt on it, till it

made her shameful petition to be impossible. She
should have said : ' But Andrew, and Peter, and all
the ten, have mothers like me. All their mothers
are just as ambitious for all their sons as I am for
mine. And they will feel toward me and toward my
sons just the same suspicion, and jealousy, and envy,
and hatred, and ill-will, that I feel toward them.
And what would I think of them if they took advantage of their friendship with Christ, as I am taking
advantage of my friendship with Him, in order to
get Him to favour them and their sons at our
expense ? And what would I think of Him if He
was imposed upon, and prevailed upon, to overlook,
and neglect, and injure my sons, at the shameful
plot of some of their mothers ? ' Had Salome talked
in that way to her own heart ; and, especially, had
she brought up her sons to look at themselves and
at all their fellows in that light ; she would then
have been as wise a woman as she now was a fool,
and as good a mother as she now was a bad. Where
had Salome lived all her days ? What kind of a
mother had she herself had ? In what synagogue
in all Israel had she worshipped God ? Who had
been her teachers in the things of God ? What had
she been thinking about all the time our Lord had
been teaching and preaching in her hearing, as He
did every day, about seeing with other people's eyes,
and feeling with other people's hearts, and doing to
other mothers and to their sons as she would have
them do to her and to her sons ? How could she
have lived in this world, and especially in the day
and in the discipleship of Christ, and how could she

have borne and brought up her sons to be His
disciples, and still be capable of this disgraceful
scheme? Had she possessed one atom of experience
of the world, not to say of truth and wisdom and
love, she could never have petitioned for a place of
such offence and such danger for her two sons. Even
if Christ had asked it of her, she would have shrunk
from exposing her two sons to the envy and the
anger and the detraction of all the ten, and of many
more besides. 'Employ my sons in Thy service,'
she would have petitioned; 'but let it be in some
secluded and obscure place. Make them Thy true
disciples even to death; but, I do beseech Thee,
if it be Thy will, hide them in the secret of Thy
presence from the pride of men, and keep them
secretly in Thy pavilion from the strife of tongues.'
She would have kneeled and worshipped and so
spoken if she had had a mother's eye and a mother's
heart in her bosom. But instead of that, this cruel
woman to her own flesh and blood was for exposing
her two sons to every possible shaft and spear of
envy, and anger, and ill-will, and injury. 'How
great they will be, if I can help it,' the heartless
creature talked to herself and said: 'What titles
they will wear! What power they will exercise!
And how all Galilee will hear of it, and how they
will all envy Salome!' Till she said: 'Leave it to
me, my sons; leave it to me.' And James and John
left it to her, and they both knelt down beside her
as she said: 'Lord, I have a certain thing to ask of
Thee.'

It was our Lord's continual way to make Scriptures out of His disciples, and to have those Scriptures written and preserved for our edification. And He made this Scripture for us out of Salome and James and John and the ten; this solemn Scripture: "It must needs be that offences come, but woe to that man by whom the offence cometh!" Woe to Salome and to her two sons, that is, for she made herself a great offence to the ten that day. She would have been offence enough simply with her so-near relationship to Christ, and with her so-gifted and so-privileged sons. But not content with that, she must needs take and lay both her sons as sheer rocks of offence right in the way of the headlong ten. Just because she was His mother's sister; just because James and John were His cousins; she and they should have kept in the background of the discipleship, and should never have come out of that background but with tender and slow and softly-taken steps. But it will take all the tremendous disenchantment of the coming Thursday and Friday to bring James and John and the others to their sober senses. And oh! you who are not come to your sober senses yet, with all Salome's shame all written for that purpose,—what, in the name of God, is to bring you to yourself? Oh, born fools and blind, not to see what stumbling-stones and what rocks of offence you are to other men, just as they are to you! Not to see the broken bones that other men take from you, just as surely as you take the same from them. Salome could not help it that she was His mother's sister. And James and John could not help it that they were their mother's sons. And you may be as blameless and as innocent as they were in that, and yet you may be a stone of stumbling down to death and hell to many men around you. At every talent that has been committed to you; at every added talent that you make for yourself and for the Church and for Christ; at every sweet word of praise that sounds around your honoured name; at every step you are summoned to take up to higher service; there are men all around you eyeing you with an evil eye. It is the same evil eye, with the same javelin in it, that Saul threw at David. It is the same evil eye with which both Peter and Judas shot hatred that day at James and John. And all the time, and till the javelin sang past their heads and stuck fast in the wall just beyond them, the two besotted brothers were in uttermost ignorance of what they and their mother had done, and what they had led the ten into doing, and what shame and pain they had caused their clear-eyed and pure-hearted Master. And even had James and John got their two thrones, would they, do you think, have got one-thousandth part of the pleasure out of their thrones that Peter and the nine would have got pain? And your own cup of honour, and praise, and what not, is not half so sweet to you as it is bitter as blood to the Peters and the Judases who see it in your hand. There is nothing but the merest and the sourest dregs in your cup, but they who see it at your lips do not know that. "It is impossible but that offences will come; but woe unto him through whom they come!"

LXXXIII

THE WIDOW WITH THE TWO MITES

SHE was a widow. And she was surely the poorest widow in all the city that day. But she had this—that she was rich toward God, and that He was rich toward her. For she loved the house of God. She was another Anna. Only, Anna lodged in the precincts of the temple, and departed not from the temple night and day, whereas this poor widow somehow and somewhere had an impoverished house of her own. "O God, thou art my God," she kept saying to herself all the way up from her own impoverished house with the two mites in her hand; "my soul shall be satisfied as with marrow and fatness; and my mouth shall praise Thee with joyful lips, when I remember Thee upon my bed, and meditate on Thee in the night watches." When one after another of her neighbours and her kindred railed on her for going up to the Court of the Women in her deep poverty, she answered them not again. Only, she did not turn back, nor did she lose hold of her two mites. "Two mites," says Mark, "make a farthing." She had no great temptation to let her left hand know what her right hand intended to do. And thus it was that without once lifting her eyes off the temple steps she cast her contribution into the temple-chest, and passed on into the temple to offer her morning prayer, and then went down to her own house. She had seen nobody, she had spoken to nobody, and nobody had seen or spoken to her. And she does not know to this day what we know. Nor will she know till that day when everything shall be known and made manifest. What would she have thought if she had been told Who had watched her that day, and what He had said about her, and that we would be reading about her to-night in this far-off island of the sea? As also that her two mites would multiply, all down the ages, into millions upon millions of gold and silver, the same Eyes still watching the process all the time? And what will she think and what will she say when all that is told from the housetop on that day about her, and about her two mites, by the Judge of all? And still He sits over against the treasury in this temple to-night, and calls unto Him His disciples among us, and says to us, 'Verily I say unto you also.' And as He sits and speaks to us, and points us to this poor widow, we lay to heart from Him many lessons.

In every department of merely secular finance money is just money. The Chancellor of Her Majesty's Exchequer does not care one straw what our feelings toward him and toward his office are when he sends us in our income-tax schedule. He does not interrogate us as to our political principles, or even as to our loyalty to the throne. Only pay your taxes promptly and he will not trouble you again till next year. But it was very different from that in those communities where Paul was the collector of the contributions of the apostolic churches. "Brethren," he wrote, "we do you to wit of the grace of God bestowed on the churches of Macedonia, who first gave themselves to the Lord. For ye know the grace of our Lord Jesus Christ, that, though He was rich, yet for your sakes He became poor. Therefore, see that ye abound in this grace also." And, as our Lord sat over against the thirteen chests in the temple that day, and all thirteen for the temple upkeep in one way or another, it was not the money so much as the mind of the contributors that He watched and weighed. And thus it was that this poor widow's mind weighed out for her this never-to-be-forgotten approval and applause of our Lord, "Verily I say unto you, that this poor widow hath cast more in than all they which have cast into the treasury." Because, as Paul has it, she had first cast in herself. That, then, is our first and fundamental lesson in all church finance. It is ourselves first; and then, after ourselves, it is our time, and our money, and our work. Two mites of mind and intention outweigh out of sight a million of mere money in the balances of the sanctuary.

"For if there be first a willing mind, it is accepted according to that a man hath, and not according to that he hath not." And thus it comes about that such a noble and ennobling equality is established in the Church of Christ. Why, our very Lord Himself, though He was rich, yet for our sakes had become so poor that the poor widow was richer than He was that day. He had absolutely nothing; not so much as two mites, to call His own that day. He had literally and absolutely nothing but a willing mind. And thus it was that He sat so near the treasury enjoying the sight of the liberality of those who had both the willing mind and money also. He had no money. He had only Himself. And as they cast in their money, He again cast in Himself. All the time the poor widow was coming up the street singing to her own heart the sixty-third Psalm, our Lord was sitting in the treasury singing to His Father the fortieth Psalm. "Sacrifice and offering Thou didst not desire. Mine ears hast thou opened; burnt offering and sin offering hast Thou not required. Then said I, Lo, I come. In the volume of the book it is written of me, I delight to do Thy will, O my God; yea, Thy law is within my heart." I have an ancient friend in this congregation who, also, has God's law in this respect within her heart. Like Paul's Macedonian saints she has very little more than a willing mind. She puts on her old bonnet once a year and is announced into my study with five shillings in her hand. Where she gets it I cannot imagine, but this is what she does with it. I have another fellow-communicant who calls on me annually with a pound. But the five-shilling one touches me most. For her little room looks to me when I visit it as if she had far more need, not of five shillings, but of five pounds every year either

from me or from the poor's box. But she has
always a clean chair and a cup of tea for me when
I call to see her. "A shilling," she said to me the
other day when she came on her annual errand, "for
Armenia. A shilling for the Jewish schools in
Constantinople. A shilling for the miners' mission.
A shilling for the Zenana ladies. And a shilling,
over and above Dr. Chalmers's penny a week, for the
Sustentation Fund." I would be a brute if I refused
to take it. I would have yet to learn the first
principles of the grace of God if I were tempted to
say to her to take it away and to buy coals with it.
For all the coals in the bowels of all the earth
would not warm her heart and mine; and, shall I
not say it, her Master's heart, as her love for these
causes of His warms His heart, and hers, and her
minister's heart. A well-to-do worshipper sent me
the other day a hundred pounds as a special donation, over and above the hundred he gives in monthly
instalments to his deacon. For more reasons than
the coming dividend in May I was mightily delighted
with his noble and timeous donation. But the five
shillings melted my heart far more. He who sits
over against His treasury here also, will Himself tell
you in your hearing that day what He has to say
about these two, and all such like princely minds.
"That"—it was said by a great preacher in a land
of vineyards and olive yards in illustration and in
enforcement of this very same subject of a willing
mind—"that which comes from His people at the
gentle pressure of their Lord's simple bidding, comes
as the fine and sweet and golden-coloured olive oil

"Our very Lord Himself, though He was rich, yet for our sakes had become so poor that the poor widow was richer than He was that day."

which runs freely from the fruit, almost before the press has ever touched it. That, again, is as the dark and coarse dregs, which is wrung out by the force of a harsh constraint at the last." "When I was in France," says Bacon, "it was said of the Duke of Guise that he was the greatest usurer in all the land, because he had turned all his estates into obligations; meaning that he had left himself nothing, but only had bound great numbers of persons in life-long indebtedness to him." It is not for the lip of mortal man to say it, but it is true, that Almighty God holds Himself under obligations to us all, corresponding to all the estates, great or small, that we have spent upon Him and upon His house. And if it is only the inward estate of a more and more willing mind, what usurers we are, and what an obligation will He acknowledge and repay!

Mutatis mutandis, as the Latin lawyers said; making all allowance, that is, for the immense change of dispensation and of all other circumstances, the thirteen temple-chests of our Lord's day were just the Endowment Funds, and the Augmentation Funds, and the Sustentation Funds of our own land and day. There were special chests elsewhere in the temple for the poor, and for the education of the children of the poor, but the treasury chests over against which our Saviour sat that day were just the Deacons' Courts of our own Free Church and other churches. It is doing no exegetical or homiletical violence to this exquisite scene to transfer every syllable of it to ourselves as a

congregation and a court. Indeed it would take
some blindness of mind and some pulpit ineptitude
to lead us past the outstanding lessons and applica-
tions of this delightful Scripture. For our own
Sustentation Fund is just that very same temple
treasury over again exactly. By means of those
chests the temple worshippers by their daily and
weekly and monthly and yearly contributions sup-
ported the priests, the doctors, the readers of the
law, and all the other office-bearers of the sanctuary.
And, like our Sustentation Fund also, all classes
contributed to the support of the sacred house;
from the rich among the people down to this poor
widow. Just as with ourselves where some give to
this one fund hundreds of pounds a year and others
a penny a week. And then out of our great central
fund an equal dividend is made every May to every
minister of the Free Church, from John O'Groats
to Maidenkirk. So much so, that wherever you see
a Free Church door open on a Sabbath morning, in
town or country, and the people flocking up to it,
you have had a hand in opening that door, and
in sustaining that minister, and in preaching the
unsearchable riches of Christ to that congregation.
And if, under God's hand, you are such a widow
that you have nothing to give to your deacon but
a willing mind, and a word of God-speed, that is
quite enough. You are a rich contributor and a
true pillar of the Free Church. It is no irreverence,
but only a becoming gratitude and love to say it,
that as I sit at the head of the monthly table of
our Deacons' Court I have something in my heart

not unlike what was in His heart who sat that day in the treasury of the temple. As I see our deacons coming in and laying down on the table, one a few shillings, and another hundreds of pounds, like Him I rejoice at the sight, and a little like Him I hope, I give myself again to the service of God and to the service of His people. If you could all see, as I every first Monday of every month see, our splendidly-equipped and splendidly-managed Deacons' Court, the sight would both move, and inflame, and sanctify your heart also. Tens and twenties of the finest young fellows in the city; arts, law, medical, and divinity students; young merchants, young bankers, young advocates, young tradesmen, — all tabling the income of their districts, and all received with the applause of the elders sitting around. And if you could hear the treasurer's monthly report, and then the censor's so stringent monthly scrutiny, and then the thanks-giving psalms and prayers, you would give far more to this so sustaining and so sanctifying Fund than you have yet given. And you would see, not by any means to perfection, but to a certain honest approximation, what a modern treasury-chest of the Lord's house ought to be, and what it will yet be in every congregation in the coming days of the Church of Christ in Scotland. For it is not by any means the enormous wealth of this congregation that has given to Free St. George's its honourable place at the head of this honourable Fund. It is, I shall say it in your presence, the exceptional intelligence in church matters and in personal religion that has all along, with all its drawbacks, characterised Dr. Andrew Thomson's and Dr. Candlish's congregation. And, taken along with all that, its absolutely unique and unapproached Deacons' Court.

LXXXIV

PONTIUS PILATE

T was Pontius Pilate who crucified our Lord. But for Pontius Pilate our Lord would not have been crucified. In spite of Pontius Pilate our Lord might have been stoned to death before the palace of the high priest that passover morning. Or, lest there should be an uproar among the people, He might have been fallen upon and murdered when He was on His knees in the garden of Gethsemane that passover night. The assassins of the city might have covenanted with Caiaphas that they would neither eat bread nor drink water till they had killed Jesus of Nazareth. The whole council of the scribes, and the elders, and the chief priests had finally determined that Jesus of Nazareth, one way or another, must be put to death; but, with all that, it was Pontius Pilate who put Him to the death of the cross.

Pontius Pilate was the Roman governor. He was the Roman procurator placed at that time over Judah and Jerusalem. He was Cæsar's representative and viceroy. What Tiberius himself was in

I

Rome, all that Pontius Pilate was in Jerusalem. The Emperor Tiberius had made a special selection of Pontius Pilate, and had sent him east with special instructions to govern, with his very best ability, the very difficult province of Judea. Pilate's was a much-coveted post among his rivals in Rome, but he had not found it to be a bed of roses. For, as the Jews had been the hardest to conquer, so had they continued to be the hardest to hold down, of all the races that ever writhed under Cæsar's heel. The conquest of Jerusalem, and the military occupation and civil management of that city and the surrounding country, cost the Roman Empire far more men and far more administrative anxiety than all that Jewry was ever worth. But the Roman statesmanship was not to be baffled, nor were the Roman eagles to be chased out of Jerusalem, by that malignant remnant of the Hebrew race. And thus it was that a procurator of such sleepless vigilance and such relentless temper as Pontius Pilate was selected and sent out to mingle the blood of all Jewish insurrectionaries with their sacrifices. And it had demanded all Pilate's personal astuteness, and all his practised statecraft, and it had called forth no little of his proverbial cruelty also, in order to stamp out one outbreak of the insurgent Jews after another. Till it would be hard to tell which of the two was by this time the more exasperated at the other: Pontius Pilate at the rulers of Jerusalem, or the rulers of Jerusalem at Pontius Pilate. The rage and the revenge of the rulers of Jerusalem against Pontius Pilate burn to this day like coals of juniper in the pages both of Philo and of Josephus.

But of all the problems and responsibilities that had arisen in his province during Pilate's procuratorship, nothing had so much perplexed him, nothing had put him so completely out of his depth, as this widespread and mysterious movement originated by John of Jerusalem, and carried on by Jesus of Nazareth. Pilate had often wished that he could detect one single atom of danger to the Roman domination in John or in Jesus, or in any of their disciples, or in any of their doctrines or practices. But, absolute wolf for Jewish blood as Pilate always was, he was not wicked enough nor wolf enough to murder an innocent man merely because he could not comprehend him.

'Divine and Most Illustrious Tiberius,' so ran one of Pilate's procuratorial reports about this time, ' all is quiet here. I have had my troubles with ' this insufferable and ungovernable people, but ' neither watchfulness nor firmness has been wanting ' on my part. Only, the former matter of Jesus ' the son of David still perplexes me. I sometimes ' wish that a wiser man than I am were in my place, ' so that he might better report to you about this ' mysterious movement among this people. Had this ' Jesus been an ordinary Jewish zealot, or an insur- ' rectionary of an everyday order, my duty to my ' master would soon have been fulfilled. But, as a ' matter of fact, Jesus the Christ, as he is called, ' is worth more to my administration than any ' legion of my armed men. He is the most peace-

'able and inoffensive of men. I know what I say,
'for I have had him and his discipleship watched
'and reported on in all places and at all times. Not
'only so, but it was only last week that I deter-
'mined to be a spy upon him myself, so perplexed
'was I with all that I had heard about him. I
'accordingly most effectually disguised myself, a
'thing I had never done before, and went to
'where he dwelt and told him that I had for long
'been a secret disciple of his. I am come by night,
'I told him, for fear of his enemies and mine.
'But instead of his royal descent from David, or
'his Hebrew Messiahship, or any pretensions or
'expectations of his of any kind, he would speak
'to me about nothing and about no one—David
'nor Solomon, Cæsar nor Caiaphas—but only about
'myself. Jew, or Roman, or whatever I was, I
'must be born again, he insisted. I must be
'baptized in Jordan, confessing my sins. Till I
'was so born again, I, like all men, loved the dark-
'ness rather than the light, because my deeds were
'evil. And, that the only way to know the truth,
'and to be sure of the truth, and not to be afraid or
'ashamed of the truth, was just to do my duty to the
'truth, and to do nothing else. And when I asked
'him why he did not leave this so untruthful and so
'unfriendly land, and go and open a philosopher's
'school about all these things in Rome or Athens
'or Alexandria, his only reply to me was that he
'was not sent but to the lost sheep of the house of
'Israel. And, then, his eyes and his hands as he
'dismissed me from his presence were absolutely the

' eyes and the hands of a king. I shall not lift
' a single finger against this " King of the Jews,"
' as his disciples call him, till I am commanded by
' Cæsar so to do.'

Well, it was while Pontius Pilate's procuratorial
despatch was still on its way to Rome that the case
contained in it came to a head in Jerusalem. It
was the morning of the passover, and it was still
early, when Jesus of Nazareth, with His hands
bound behind His back, was led up by the whole
Sanhedrim to Pilate's judgment-seat. As soon as
he had sat down on his seat of judgment-Pilate
demanded of the rulers of Jerusalem, " What accusation bring ye against this man?" They answered
and said, ' If he were not a malefactor, and indeed
deserving of the death of the cross, we would not
have brought him before thee. We found this
fellow perverting the people and forbidding the
people to give tribute to Cæsar, saying that he
himself is Christ a king, and the Son of God.'
When Pilate heard that, he took the prisoner apart,
and asked Him, " Whence art Thou?" Pilate's
heart was made of Roman iron, and his Roman
heart had never failed him before. But, altogether;
what with all he had heard and seen of our Lord
already; and what with all he heard and saw of Him
that morning; Pilate's heart absolutely stood still
as he ventured to put to Him the staggered
question: " Whence art Thou?" And Pilate's
secret fear became downright terror when his
prisoner looked up at him with such eyes, but
answered him nothing. It was at that very moment

that Pilate's wife exclaimed to her husband : 'How
dreadful is this Roman prætorium to me this passover morning! Let us arise and return to Cæsarea!
Have thou nothing to do with this just man, for I
have suffered many things this whole past night in
dreams and in visions because of him!' Just what
shape her great sufferings had taken all that night
we are not told. She, too, may have had reports
brought to her about the preaching of John and
Jesus. She, too, may have had her spies set upon
Him. She, too, may have had told her some of
His tremendous sermons that very passover week.
For all Jerusalem—from top to bottom—was ring-
ing with those terrible passover parables of His,
And, out of all that she had seen and heard and
apprehended,—what sufferings may not have come
to Pilate's wife in her divinely-ordered dream that
so awful night? She may have seen the Son of
Man coming in His glory, and all His holy angels
with Him. And she may have seen the kings of
the earth, and the great men, and the rich men,
and the mighty men, and her husband among them,
hiding themselves in the dens and in the rocks of
the mountains: and saying to the mountains and
the rocks, Fall on us, and hide us from the face of
Him that sitteth on the throne. 'Have thou
nothing to do with that just man,' she said, 'for I
have suffered some fearful sights this night because
of Him!' "Wife," said the gaoler of Derby, with
a doleful voice, "I have seen the day of judgment:
and I saw George Fox there, and I was afraid of
him, because I had done him so much wrong, and

had spoken so much against him in the taverns and the alehouses."

With all his heart would Pilate have fallen in with his wife's warning, had it been possible for him to do so. He did not need her urgent message. He knew far better than she did that the prisoner at his bar was a just man, and something more than a just man, but that only tied up Pilate's hands all the tighter. " Have thou nothing to do with that just man!" Yes; but how is Pilate to get rid of that just man, hunted to death as both that just man and his judge both are by those inhuman hyænas who fill the palace court with their bloodthirsty cries? 'Tell me,' was Pilate's despairing reply to his trembling wife; 'tell me how I am to wash my hands of this just man: tell me how I am to set him free, and at the same time to satisfy his enemies, who have both him and me in their power?' But as their clamour still went on Pilate caught at one of their cries and thought he saw in it a loop-hole for himself at any rate, if not for his prisoner. "He stirreth up the people from Galilee to this place!" they cried. Now, as Pilate's good planet would have it, who should be in Jerusalem that passover morning but Herod Antipas, under whose jurisdiction all Galilee was, and Jesus therefore, as a Galilean. And the tetrarch was vastly pleased with the un- expected recognition of his royal sceptre, when this Galilean prisoner was sent by Pilate to receive Herod's sentence on him. And all the more so, that Pilate and Herod had had so many quarrels together about this very matter of Herod's jurisdiction. But

here is the Roman governor, in his own city, and
at his own instance, recognising in the most open and
handsome way the too-oft invaded rights and pre-
rogatives of the king of Galilee. "And the same
day," says the Evangelist, "Pilate and Herod were
made friends together again." And made friends,
as that poor fox little knew, at such a cheap price
on Pilate's part! But Pilate was not to get so easily
rid of our Lord as all that. Herod Antipas was
more of a circus-master than a serious-minded
monarch; and, instead of taking up the case that
had been referred to his jurisdiction, all that Herod
aimed at was to get some amusement out of the
accused. 'He is the King of the Jews, is he? He
is a candidate for my royal seat, is he? Then put
the white coat of a candidate upon him, and send
him back to Pilate. The Governor will enjoy my
jest: and it will somewhat cement our recovered
friendship!'

It is impossible for us to enter into all our Lord's
thoughts as He was dragged up and down the streets
of Jerusalem that passover morning. Dragged in
cords from Gethsemane to Caiaphas, and from
Caiaphas to Pilate, and from Pilate to Herod, and
from Herod back again to Pilate. And all the
time with all the shame and insult heaped upon
Him that the evil hearts of His enemies could devise.
Our Lord's thoughts and feelings at all times are a
great deep to us. But Pilate was a man of like
passions with ourselves, and we can quite well understand what his thoughts and his feelings were when
the chief priests were back again with their prisoner

at the prætorium. What is Pilate to do? With all
his power and with all his diplomacy what is Pilate
to do next? You all know what he did next. He
put up Jesus to the vote of the people against
Barabbas, trusting that the gratitude and the pity
and the sense of fairplay among the common people
would carry the day. But, difficult as it is to
explain, they all suddenly turned round and cried
out with one voice, "Away with Him! Away with
Him, and release to us Barabbas!" "Why?"
demanded Pilate, with indignation and exasperation, 'What evil has this man ever done? Neither
Herod nor I have found the shadow of a fault in
Him.' You have seen the vote taken at an election-
time in your own city. And you have seen how ill-
will, and envy, and personal spite are so much more
active at such times than justice, and gratitude, and
goodness, and truth. Ignorance, and prejudice, and
pure maliciousness, will come out to the polling-
booth on their crutches and will need neither your
canvasser nor your carriage to come for them. "Not
this man, but Barabbas!" cried the rulers of the
Jews; and to a man the rabble of the people cried
out with them, "Away with Him! Away with Him!
Crucify Him! Crucify Him!"

Whatever the wicked spirit may have been that
took possession of the populace of Jerusalem that
awful passover morning, the Holy Ghost Himself
witnesses to us that it was the wickedest spirit in all
hell that had come up and had taken possession of
Caiaphas and his colleagues now for a long time.
And we knew it before it was told us. We have

seen it coming all the time. And Pilate saw it
that morning, and had seen it coming all the time,
and had told Tiberius about it. Our Lord's life
and teaching and wonderful works, and the multitudes that were attracted to Him by all that;—it
would have been the New Jerusalem above, and
Caiaphas would have been a sanctified saint in
heaven, not to have had his heart burned up with
envy within him at our Lord's popularity with the
people. It is at this moment in the Passion Play at
Ober-Ammergau that the chorus comes forward
with this warning to us:

> 'Tis envy—which no mercy knows,
> In which hell's flame most fiercely glows—
> Lights this devouring fire.
> All's sacrificed unto its lust—
> Nothing too sacred, good, or just
> To fall to its desire.
> Oh ! woe to those this passion sweeps
> Helpless and bound into the deeps !

Pilate had never heard of the Jerusalem that is
above, but no man knew better than he did the
Jerusalem that was yelling like all the furies all
around him. Caiaphas had put on his holiest of
masks that holiest of mornings, and he had demanded swift execution to be done on this traitor
against Cæsar and this blasphemer against God.
But Pilate was not a child. Heathen as Pilate
was, and hardened as a stone in his heart as he was,
he both saw down into, and despised and detested
every high priest, and scribe, and elder of them all.
It was a noble hyperbole that was put upon Plato's

tombstone: "Here lies a man too good and too great for envy." But that literally true epitaph, and no hyperbole, could not have been written even on Joseph's new tomb as long as Caiaphas remained alive in Jerusalem. Our Lord Himself was neither too good nor too great for Caiaphas's envy and ill-will, nor for Pilate's selfish cowardice and open sale of truth and justice. For, all this time, with all his power, and with all his pride, and with all his astuteness, and with all his resource, the chain of his terrible fate was fast closing around Pontius Pilate. And his rage, and his pain, and his pride drove him well-nigh demented. Never, surely, since mortal man was first taken and held fast in the snare of Satan, was any miserable man more completely seized and carried captive of his past sins and his present circumstances, than Pontius Pilate was that passover morning. And it all came to a head, and the fatal chain was all riveted round Pilate for the last time, when the savage threat was spat up at him: "If thou let this man go, thou art not Cæsar's friend!" That was enough. For at that Pilate took water, in his defeat and despair, and washed his hands before the multitude, and said: 'I, at any rate, am innocent of the blood of this just person: See ye, his murderers, to it.' And they saw to it.

All that is not the half of the history of that awful morning to Pontius Pilate, and of all that he went through. But that is enough to set Pilate sufficiently before our eyes in the hour and power of his fatal temptation. And all that is told us in order that we may turn our eyes inward and ask

ourselves what we would have done that passover
morning had we been in Pilate's place; had we
stood between the deadly anger of Cæsar at us on
the one hand, and with only a just man to be
scourged and crucified on the other hand! We
would have done just what Pilate did. To protect
ourselves; to stand well with our masters, and to
preserve our paying post; we would have washed
our hands, and would have scourged Jesus, righteous
man and all.   Who here, and in this hour of truth,
will dare to cast a stone at Pontius Pilate? What
self-seeking, what self-sheltering, what truth-selling,
what soul-selling man?

> O break, O break, hard heart of mine !
>   Thy weak self-love and guilty pride
> His Pilate and His Judas were :
>   Jesus, our Lord, is crucified !

I know all the old legends, sacred and profane,
about Pontius Pilate, and about his miserable end.
But I shall not believe any of them.   I shall continue
to hope against hope for poor Pontius Pilate.   If my
sale of my Saviour, and of my own soul, has so often
chased me up to the Cross of Christ, so I think
Pilate's remorse must have chased him.   And as he
washed his hands in water that passover morning,
so I shall hope he washed his hands and his heart ten
thousand times in after days in that Fountain for sin
which he had such an awful hand in opening.   The
world would not contain the books if all the names
of all the chief priests, and scribes, and inhabitants
of Jerusalem; and all the governors, and centurions,

and soldiers of Rome, who came to believe on Christ
crucified were to be written in them. " Ye men
of Israel, hear these words: Jesus of Nazareth, a
man approved of God, Him ye have taken, and by
wicked hands have crucified and slain. And now,
brethren, I wot that through ignorance ye did it,
as did also your rulers. But unto you first, God,
having raised up His Son Jesus, has sent Him to
bless you, in turning away every one of you from his
iniquities." Who can tell? With that glorious
Gospel preached far and wide, and with the Redeemer's prayer offered with His own blood to back
it on the Cross, Father, forgive them : who can tell?
I, for one, shall continue to hope for Pontius Pilate,
as for myself. For—

> O love of God ! O sin of man !
>   In this dread act your strength is tried,
> And victory remains with love :
>   Jesus, our Lord, is crucified !

LXXXV

PILATE'S WIFE

OUR men of natural science are able some-times to reconstruct the shape and the size of a completely extinct species from a single bone, or splinter of a bone, that has been quite accidentally dug out of the earth. And in something of the same way Pilate's wife rises up before us out of a single sentence in Matthew's Gospel. We see the governor's wife only for a moment. We hear her only for a moment. But in the space of that short moment of time she so impresses her sudden foot-print on this page of this Gospel, that as long as this Gospel is read, this that Pilate's wife said and did that Passover morning shall be held in remem-brance for a most honourable memorial of her.

Both Pilate and his wife, in Paul's words, were Gentiles in the flesh, being aliens from the common-wealth of Israel, and strangers from the covenants of promise, having no hope, and without God in the world. Both Pilate and his wife were perfect heathens, as we would say. They were still at what we would call the pre-patriarchal period of

divine revelation. They were still very much what
Abraham himself was when God chose him, and
spake to him, and said to him, "Get thee out of
thy country, and from thy kindred, and from thy
father's house, unto a land that I will show thee."
As regards many of the good things of this life;
learning, civilisation, refinement, and such like; the
Roman governor and his gifted wife were very far
advanced; but as regards what our Lord estimates
to be the one thing needful for all men, they were
not unlike Terah, and Nahor, and Abram, when
they still dwelt in old time on the other side of the
flood, and still served other gods. Both Pilate and
his wife were still at that stage in which God was
wont to speak to men at sundry times and in divers
manners; and, among other manners, in the manner
of a dream. For, till Holy Scripture came to some
fulness and to some clearness, we find God revealing
Himself in a dream, not only to Abraham, and
Pharaoh, and Nebuchadnezzar; but even to Jacob,
and Joseph, and Solomon, and down even to such
New Testament men as Peter, and Paul, and John.
Almighty God has complete control and continual
command of all the avenues that lead into the soul
of man, and He sends His message to this soul and
to that at the very time and in the very way that
seems wisest and best in His sight. And Elihu's
remarkable description of the manner and the matter
of one of his own divine dreams may be taken as a
prophetic forecast of this passover dream of Pilate's
wife: "In a dream, in a vision of the night, when
deep sleep falleth upon men, in slumberings upon the

bed: then He openeth the ears of men, and sealeth
their instruction, that He may withdraw man from
his purpose, and hide pride from man. He keepeth
back his soul from the pit, and his life from
perishing by the sword. He is chastened also
with pain upon his bed, and the multitude of
his bones with strong pain." A perfect picture
of Pilate's wife's dream in the Prætorium that
night, and of its divinely-intended purpose toward Pilate himself, which was to withdraw Pilate
from his purpose, and to keep back his soul from
the pit.

Long before that passover morning Pilate's wife
had made up her mind about Jesus of Nazareth.
With all the wealth and all the rank of the city
against Him; with all the temple learning and all
the temple authority against Him; with, without
exception, every responsible ruler and every influential man in all Jerusalem against Him; and with
all her own and all her husband's original interests
and natural instincts strongly prejudicing her against
Him—she had overcome all that, and had deliberately and resolutely taken up His side. She had
made up her mind that whatever else He was, or
might turn out to be, at any rate up to the present
moment, He had been a blameless man. He had
gone about doing good. The procurator's palace
was the centre and the seat of everything. All the
telegraph wires ran up and delivered themselves
there. Everything that took place in the province
was instantly reported at the Prætorium. Not a
word of rebellion was whispered in closets, not a

zealot stirred a foot in the greatest stealth, not a
sword was sharpened at midnight in all the land,
but it was all as well known to Pilate and to his wife
as to the intending insurrectionary himself. And,
though the Roman procurators were wont to leave
their wives at home when they set out to their pro-
vinces, Pilate's wife was far too meet a help to him
to be left behind him when he was wrestling for his
life with those rebellious and treacherous Jews in
Jerusalem. And it was so. The procurator's wife
shared all her husband's anxieties, all his responsibilities, and all his apprehensions. She was with
him in everything with her keen mind and her noble
heart. And with all her swift divination she had
come to the sure conclusion long ago that Jesus of
Nazareth was all and more than He seemed to be.
Her Hebrew maid could not assist her Roman
mistress to dress, but, one way or other, the same
subject of conversation continually came up—what
He had last said, and what He had last done. She
could not drive out through the gate of the city but
there was His congregation covering the highway.
She could not return home that He was not healing
some sick man at the door of the temple. And, all
that passover week,—what with her husband's spies,
and what with her own, she knew as well as Annas
and Caiaphas themselves knew what they had determined to do. She had watched out of her window
what we now know as the entry into Jerusalem.
She had heard coming over the valley the voices of
the children in the temple crying out and saying,
" Hosanna to the Son of David ! " till she wished

K

that her children were among them. The last thing
that absolutely carried her whole heart captive was
Martha and Mary and their brother Lazarus. And
it had needed all her own self-command, and all her
husband's command over her as her husband, to
keep her from going out to Bethany to see Lazarus
with her own eyes. She had often read of such
things in her own ancient books at home, but such
a thing as this had never come so near her before.
And then, when the report came to the Prætorium
that Lazarus's friend had been betrayed and taken
prisoner, and was all that night to be under trial
before Caiaphas and the council; and then, that
it would all roll in upon her husband the next
morning—if a dream cometh through the multitude of business—no wonder that Pilate's wife
dreamed about Jesus of Nazareth all that passover
night!

Just what shape her dream took that passover
night, I would give something for myself to know.
And it is not mere and idle curiosity that makes
me say that, for it would be to me a great lesson
in the first principles of divine revelation to the
Old Testament Church, as well as to this Roman
matron's soul, and to my own soul. It would be
as good as another disinterred manuscript of the
Acts of Pilate, did we know something of the
multitude of this business about Jesus that had
gone that night to make up that so suffering and
so opportune dream. With the books of the
Hebrew prophets on her table, and with the echoes
of John's preaching and Jesus' parables filling the

air all around her, what may the governor's wife
not have seen and heard in the visions and voices of
that ominous night? She may have seen a hand
coming out and writing it on the wall of the Prætorium, " Mene, Mene, Tekel, Upharsin." She may
have seen the same sight that made Daniel himself
to be troubled, and his countenance to change.
She may have seen the Ancient of days, with His
throne like the fiery flame, and His wheels as burning fire, and the judgment set, and the books
opened. She may have seen one like the Son of
Man come with the clouds of heaven, till His
kingdom was an everlasting kingdom, and His
dominion that shall not be destroyed. Till, 'For
God's sake,' she said, ' have thou nothing to do with
that dreadful man?' Now, among all your dreams
and visions on your bed do you ever dream about
Jesus Christ? You dream every night about this
man and that woman that you love or hate. Do
you ever dream about your Saviour? Do you love
and fear Him to that extent? If He were actually
engaged within you on the salvation of your soul,
the multitudinous business connected with that
inward work would surely make you think about
Him all day till you would dream about Him all
night. Do you ever do it? Will you be able to
say to Him at the last day, 'Lord, Thou knowest
that I often thought about Thee all day and dreamed
about Thee all night, and told my husband my
dreams about Thee in the morning?' Will you
have as much as Pilate's heathen wife will have
to say for herself and for him? Will you; or

will you not? What do you think? What do you say?

And then, this will be openly acknowledged and admitted in the day of judgment that Pilate's wife was fearlessly true and faithful to all her light. Her best light was as yet but candle-light. It was but as rush-light. But, even candle-light, even rush-light, even the faintest reflection of candle-light or rush-light is, all the time, the very same light as the light of the noonday sun. All light of all kinds comes, in one way or another, from one and the same source. And the lurid light of Pilate's wife's dream that night all came to her and to him from the Light of the world. The identical same Light that is lighting you and me with such brilliance and beauty in this house to-night, that very same Light struggled within that Roman lady's soul on her bed and in her dreams in Jerusalem that night. And nothing in divine things is more sure than this, that they who love the light—be it candle-light or be it sun-light—shall have more light sent to them, till they have all the light that they need. To them their path shall shine more and more to the perfect day. They who love the light, and walk in what light they have, they shall never lie down in darkness. You may absolutely depend upon it that the True Light Himself, who stood under such a cloud before Pilate's bar that daybreak, both overheard and laid up in His heart the noble message that came out to the procurator. You may rely on it that He who had already sent her so much of His own light, continued to send her more, till she became one of those princess-saints of Cæsar's household, whom Paul so saluted in long after days. And may we not hope that Pilate himself was at last completely won with the holy walk of his wife, as he beheld her chaste conversation coupled with fear?

LXXXVI

HEROD THAT FOX

JACOB BEHMEN says that a man is sometimes like a wolf, cruel and merciless, and with an insatiable thirst for blood; sometimes like a dog, snappish, malicious, envious, grudging, as a dog is with a bone that he cannot himself eat; sometimes like a serpent, stinging and venomous, slanderous in his words, and treacherous in his actions; sometimes like a hare, timorous and starting off; sometimes like a toad, and sometimes like a fox, and so on. The Teutonic philosopher has a whole incomparable chapter on " The Bestial Manifestations in Man." " My dear children in Christ," he proceeds, " my sole purpose in writing in this way to you is not to revile you or to reproach you with your fallen and bestialised estate. What I here write to you is the simple and naked and open truth. I am as certain as I live that it is the truth of God, because I have the daily experience of it all in myself. Every day, and every hour of every day, I have the bondage of it all, and the shame of it all, and the degradation and the guilt of it all, in myself, and not in another.

And, therefore, your embruted estate is here told you not to exclude any of you from the hope of salvation. The most wolf-like man among you, the most dog-like man among you, the most toad-like man among you, the most fox-like man among you —all such men are invited, and, indeed, commanded, to arise every moment and flee from themselves into the new birth in God. And, moreover, it was for this very purpose that the Son of God was manifested. It was to turn us all from being beasts and devils everlastingly, and to make us all with Himself, the new and born-from-above sons and daughters of the living God. Jesus Christ, the very Mouth of Truth Himself, called Herod a fox, not to sentence him, and to fix him for ever the fox that he was, but it was in order, if possible, to turn him from all his guiles, and all his lusts, and all his lies, and to make him even yet a child of God, and an heir of everlasting life." So writes "the illuminated Behmen" in his *Election of Grace*.

All the historians and all the biographers of that time, both sacred and profane, agree about Herod Antipas. They all agree that Antipas was his father's son in all that was worst in his father's character. Old Herod, with all his brutalities and with all his devilries, had at the same time some of the possibilities in him that go to the making of a great man. But by no possibility could his second son ever have been a great man. Antipas was a weak, cruel, sensual, ostentatious, shallow-hearted creature. He is known to the readers of the New Testament first as the dupe of a bad woman, and

then as the murderer of John the Baptist, and then
as one of the judges of Jesus Christ. He was that fox
who tried to frighten our Lord to flee from His work;
and at last he was that puppet-king, and reprobate
sinner, to whom our Lord would not answer one
word. His licentious life, his family miseries, his
political manœuvres, his sycophantic and extravagant
expenditures, his ruinous defeats, both in war and
in diplomacy, his fall from his throne, and his
banishment from his kingdom, are all to be read
in the books of Josephus, who is an author altogether worthy to chronicle the deeds, and to tell
the exploits, of such a hero. Avoid giving of
characters, says Butler in his noble sermon on "The
Government of the Tongue." At the same time, as
Bengel says, the truth must sometimes be spoken,
and must sometimes be all spoken. Sometimes a
dog must be branded to all men to be a dog, and a
serpent advertised to be a serpent, and a swine to
be a swine. 'Go back,' said our Lord, 'to that fox
which sent you, and tell him what I have said about
him: tell him the name I have denounced upon
him.' And we understand and accept both what
our Lord and His two servants have said on this
subject of the giving of characters. It is a large
part of our daily lesson and discipline and duty in
this life, to be able to give the proper characters,
and to apply the proper epithets, to men and to
things; and to do that at the right time and in the
right temper. It is a large and an important part
of every preacher's office especially, to apply to
all men and to all their actions their absolutely and

fearlessly right and true names. To track out the
wolf, and the serpent, and the toad, and the fox,
in the men in whom these bestialities dwell, and
to warn all men how and where all that will end;
no minister may shrink from that. All the vices
and all the crimes of the tetrarch's miserable life,
and all the weakness and duplicity of his contemptible character, are all summed up and sealed down
on Herod Antipas in that one divine word that
day : "That fox."

But what makes Herod Antipas such a poignant
lesson to us is not that he was a fox, it is this rather,
that he began by being a fox, and ended by being
a reprobate. You know what reprobation is, my
brethren ? This is reprobation. "As soon as Pilate
knew that this prisoner belonged to Herod's jurisdiction, he sent Him to Herod, who was in Jerusalem
at that time. And Herod questioned Jesus with
many words, but He answered him nothing." That
is reprobation. It is our reprobation begun when
God answers us nothing. When, with all our
praying, and with all our reading, and with all our
inquiring, He still answers us nothing. Herod's
day of grace had lasted long, but it is now at an
end. Herod had had many opportunities, and
at one time he was almost persuaded. At one
time he was not very far from the Kingdom of
Heaven. But all that is long past. Herod had
smothered and silenced his conscience long ago, and
now he is to be for ever let alone. Nay—and let
all beginning reprobates attend to this—not only
was Herod let alone, but when he put many eager

questions to our Lord, He answered him nothing.
It is here that the real horror and the awful fascination to me of all Herod's case comes in. It is in this:
because we also go on exactly like Herod, cheating
ourselves, and thinking, poor self-entrapped foxes
that we are, that we are all the time mocking God
also, till it is too late; for God is not to be mocked
by any man. David has drawn out this solemnising
lesson, and has set it in a singularly impressive
Psalm of his, and in never-to-be-forgotten words:
" If I regard iniquity in my heart, the Lord will not
hear me." Now, it was just because this lewd and
cruel fox had so defiantly, and so flagrantly, and so
criminally, and for so long, regarded the greatest
iniquity in his heart and in his life, that now at last
when he put so many questions to our Lord He
answered him nothing. We all know the same
thing ourselves. Fox-like, Antipas-like, Doth God
see us? we say. Surely the darkness shall cover us,
we say. Just this once more, we say. At a more
convenient time I will reform myself, we say. We
take our own way and our own time, and, fox-like,
we have many tricks in our eye by which we will
escape the trap. We have all gone on in that way,
till these words of reprobation—"no answer"—describe to perfection many of us in this house to-night.
In Herod it was murder and incest, never repented
of and never forsaken, that so absolutely shut our
Lord's mouth toward Herod and toward all his
requests and all his questions. There are no controversies so dark and so terrible between God and
our souls as the murder of John the Baptist. But

God may be as silent and as angry at all our prayers
and questions and casuistries as ever He was at
Herod's. Nobody would believe, but those of us
who have come through it, the little things, the
trivial things, that will stop God's ear, and shut His
mouth, and make Him our enemy. Somewhat too
much money spent on ourselves, and somewhat too
little spent on the Church of Christ and on His poor
will do it. Too little time and strength spent in
closet and intercessory prayer will do it. A secret
ill-feeling entertained at somebody will do it. A
debt not paid and with interest will do it. A prejudice nursed and not surrendered in time will do
it. A grudge kept up will do it. An apology not
made will do it. A too long and a too free tongue
will do it. An impertinent book, and the time and
money spent upon that book will do it. A second
sleep in the morning more than is necessary will do
it. A pipeful of doubtful tobacco will do it. A
daily glass or two of inexpedient wine will do it. A
knuckle of too-savoury mutton will sometimes do it,
as Dr. Jowett was wont to say. Nobody could tell,
nobody who has not himself come through it all
could imagine or could believe if it were told them,
the triviality, and the absolute immateriality, of the
things that will in some men's cases do it. God has
kept up a life-long controversy with some of His
saints about little things that they could not put
words upon, so unlike Almighty God and so beneath
Him, as one would say, is the whole dispute. The
truth is, when Almighty God is bent upon the
absolute sanctification of some elect sinner, no auto-

biography, no *Brea,* no *Reliquiæ,* no *Grace Abounding,*
no amount of imaginative genius and a corresponding
style, could possibly convey to another man all the
controversies, great and small, that all through his
life go on between God and that elect sinner's soul.
There are some terribly predestinated saints. There
are some elections that almost consume those chosen
souls to dust and ashes in the awful furnace of their
sanctification. The apostle had this same terrible
election, and sin-consuming ambition, for his Thessa-
lonian converts. "And the very God of peace sanctify
you wholly: and I pray God your whole spirit,
and soul, and body be preserved blameless unto the
coming of our Lord Jesus Christ." You have it all
there. It is as much as to say, the very God of
peace turn a deaf ear to your most importunate and
agonising prayers, as long as there is a single speck
of sin secretly staining any part of your soul. The
very God of peace crucify every remaining lust in your
body, and every remaining affection in your spirit,
and every remaining thought, and feeling, and passion, in your soul, till you are absolutely blameless in
His consumingly holy sight. The very God of peace
empty you from vessel to vessel, and prune you to
the quivering quick, and keep you in a sevenfold-
fire, till the coming of the Great Refiner in the glory
of His Father. And, in like manner, the very God
of peace demands of you also every moment of your
time, and every mite of your money, and every word
of your mouth, and every beat of your heart. And
not till He gets all that from you will He answer
you one word; no, not for all your prayers, and all

your sweats, and all your tears. It is not lawfui
for a child of God to have it, He will say, till He
will make your disobedient life a burden to you
past bearing, a racking torture, and one long agony.
No! He denies you, till you can hear nothing in all
your conscience but these angry words with you.
No! it is not lawful for you. It is not right. It
is not safe. It is not seemly. It is not expedient.
It may be for others, but it can never now be for
you. And as long as God in your conscience says
that to you about anything whatsoever, you may
debate, and question, and pray, and seek for marks
and evidences till your dying day, but the very God
of peace will answer you nothing.

And then there is this complication also : there
are things that it is not lawful for one man to do,
that his very next-door neighbour may do every
day, and walk with God and talk with God all the
time. There are things that are unpardonable in
the sight of God in one man, but which are not only
entirely innocent and inoffensive, but are positively
virtuous and praiseworthy in another man. There
are things that will be the ruin of one man's soul,
that may all the time be the very sweetness and
strength of his neighbour's soul. I may have to
deny myself, on the pain of reprobation, every day,
what you may eat and drink every day and ask a
blessing on it. I may have to spend all the rest of
my redeemed life in this world in a daily battle and
a nightly self-examination against habits of body
and mind that you cannot so much as imagine. I
may have to sit up at my salvation every night of the

week, while you are sleeping like an innocent child.
I may have to meditate on David's Psalms continually, and on nothing else any more, while you are
doing nothing else all your time and thought but
either telling or hearing some new thing. I may
have, till the day of my death, to fight against a
slavery that makes you, in your lush liberty, say
that I am beside myself. I may have iniquities in
my heart absolutely shipwrecking all my prayers:
iniquities that even David in his very best Psalms
knew nothing about: iniquities that did not even
exist in David's day, because the Holy Ghost was
not yet given. So beset behind and before are
some New Testament men, and some men far on in
the life of grace, that God scarcely ever answers
them one word from one year's end to another.
Then king Herod questioned with Jesus in many
words; but He answered him nothing. But, sings
David, verily God hath heard me. He hath
attended to the voice of my prayer.

LXXXVII

THE PENITENT THIEF

THE two malefactors who were crucified with Christ had been ringleaders in Barabbas's robber band. And had Barabbas himself not been pardoned by Pilate that morning, he also would have carried his cross out to Calvary that day and would have been crucified upon it. But when Barabbas and his band are called thieves and robbers it is but due to them to give them the benefit of the doubt. In our noble British law and administration there is a deep and a fundamental distinction taken between ordinary criminals against all civilised society, and political criminals against this or that foreign government for the time. We give up swindlers and murderers when they flee to our shores, but we provide a safe and an honourable asylum for political refugees and state criminals, as we call them. Now all the chances are that Barabbas and his band had begun simply by being rebels against Rome, as, indeed, all the Jews were everywhere in their hearts. Though no doubt their repudiated, outlawed, exasperated, and hunted-down lives had by degrees made Barabbas and his band desperate

and reckless, till they had become in many cases
pure thieves and robbers. David in the cave of
Adullam is not a bad picture of Barabbas at the
beginning of his life of outlawry. For every one
that was in distress came to David, and every one
that was in debt, and every one that was discon-
tented, and he became a captain over them; and
there were with David about four hundred men.
Only, no doubt, David was a far better captain
than Barabbas ever was. David, no doubt, kept his
men in far better hand, till he turned them out
such splendid specimens of soldiers and mighty
men of war, and the best law-abiding citizens in all
Israel. But David had only Saul to overthrow,
whereas Barabbas had Cæsar.

The Evangelist Luke had perfect understanding
of all things from the very first. And no doubt he
knew all about the early life of Barabbas and his
band. And especially, I feel sure, he would make
every possible inquiry concerning the early days of
this remarkable man who is discovered to us in this
Gospel as the penitent thief. But it would have
been out of place in Luke to have gone into this
man's whole past life at the moment when he is
fixing all our eyes on the crucifixion of our Lord.
At the same time, it is as clear as daylight to me
that this is not the first time that this crucified
thief has seen our Lord. He knew both our Lord's
life and teaching and character quite well, though
he had cast it all behind his back all his days up
till now. He knew that our Lord had done nothing
amiss all the time that he and his companions were

fast ripening for the due reward of their deeds. There was not a Sabbath synagogue, nor a passover journey, nor a carpenter's shop, nor a tax-gatherer's booth, nor a robber's cave in all Israel where the name, and the teaching, and the mighty works of Jesus of Nazareth were not constantly discussed, and debated, and divided on. And Barabbas and his band must have had many a deliberation in their banishment about Jesus of Nazareth. Is He indeed the promised Messiah? Is He really David's Son? Is this really He who is to overcome and cast out Cæsar? If it is, we shall join His standard immediately, and He will remember us when He comes into His kingdom. Week after week, month after month, year after year, this went on till their hearts became sick and desperate within them. A hundred times Barabbas and this one and that one of his band had disguised themselves as fishermen and shepherds to come down to hear our Lord preach and to see the mighty works that He did. Nay, for anything we know, this man may at one time have been one of our Lord's disciples, quite as well as Simon Zelotes and Judas Iscariot. In his early, and enthusiastic, and patriotic days he may have been one of John's disciples. He may have seen Jesus of Nazareth baptized that day. He may have been baptized himself that day. He may have heard the Baptist say: " Behold the Lamb of God!" He may have been among the multitude who sat and heard the Sermon on the Mount. He may actually have closely companied with our Lord for a season. Till he was at last one of those who went back and walked no more with

L

Him, because our Lord would not be taken by them
and made a king. But, go back to Barabbas's band
as he did, I defy him ever to forget what he had
seen and heard down among the cities, and the
villages, and the mountain-sides, and the supper-
tables of Galilee and Jewry. This man, and many
more like him, went back to their farm, and to their
merchandise, and to their toll-booth, and to their
robber-cave, but they took with them memories, and
visions, and hearts, and consciences, they could never
forget. As we see was the case conspicuously with
this thief on the cross.

And all this went on: our Lord finishing the
work His Father had given Him to do, while
Barabbas and his band were fast ripening for their
cross; till, as God would have it, our Lord and
Barabbas, with these two of his band, were all taken
and tried, and were sentenced to be crucified all
four on the same passover morning. Now, when
a man is on his way out to his own execution he
would be more than a man if he paid much attention, to the circumstances attending the execution
of his neighbours. At the same time, this thief
was no ordinary man. 'This is Jesus of Nazareth,'
he would say to himself. 'This is the carpenter-
prophet I used to steal into His presence to hear
Him preach. I once thought to be one of His
men myself to deliver Israel.' And then as men
among ourselves do on the morning of their execution, the psalms and hymns of his boyhood came
back into his mind. Till he did not hear the
mockery and the insults of the people who filled

the streets as he went on and said to himself:
"Remember not the sins of my youth, nor my
transgressions. For thou writest bitter things
against me, and makest me to possess the iniquities of my youth. Thou puttest my feet also in
the stocks, and lookest narrowly unto all my paths;
thou settest a print upon the heels of my feet.
We lie down in our shame, and our confusion
covereth us; for we have sinned against the Lord
our God; we and our fathers, from our youth even
unto this day, and have not obeyed the voice of
the Lord our God." Till, by that time, the terrible
procession had got to Golgotha. And all the way,
as already in the high priest's palace, and in the
Prætorium, and now at Golgotha, all hell was let
loose as never before nor since. And Satan entered
into the two thieves, and into this thief also. And
no wonder that they both cursed and blasphemed
and raved and gnashed their teeth and spat upon
their crucifiers, as all crucified men always did, so
insupportable to absolute insanity was the awful
torture of crucifixion. And all the time God was
laying on His Son the iniquity of us all, and all
the time He was dumb, and opened not His mouth.
"Save Thyself and us!" the two crucified and
maddened men both cried to Him; the one in
fiendish ribaldry, and the other out of a heart in
which heaven and hell were fighting with their last
stroke for his soul. Till this one of the two thieves
at last came to himself. And the thing that made
him come to himself was this: Our Lord had
never opened His mouth. He had neither cursed,

nor gnashed His teeth, nor spat at His crucifiers and
revilers.   But, at last, He also spoke.   And it was
the same voice—the thief had never heard another
voice in all the world to compare with it!   For,
looking up into the fast-darkening heavens, our Lord
exclaimed, "Father, forgive them; for they know
not what they do."   That benediction of our blessed
Lord did more to benumb the agony of body and
mind in this thief than all the wine mingled with
myrrh the women of Jerusalem had made for him
and for his fellows to drink that morning.   "Father,
forgive them!"—it absolutely broke the thief's hard
heart to hear it.   And as his hardened companion
still reviled our Lord hanging beside him, the now
penitent thief looked across and said to his old
companion and fellow-malefactor the words that all
the world knows.

John Donne, in a Lent sermon that he preached
at Whitehall, dwells on what he calls "The despatch of the grace of God in the case of the
penitent thief." The *per saltum* character of the
thief's repentance and faith, and the full and immediate response of our Lord to his so-sudden
repentance and faith, make a fine sermon. The
kingdom of heaven suffered violence that day at
this thief's so suddenly repentant and so believing
hands. He took heaven, so to speak, at a leap
that day. The swiftness of the thief's repentance,
and faith, and confession, and pardon, and sancti-
cation, and glorification, is something very blessed
for us all to think about, and never to forget; and,
especially, those of us who must make haste and

lose no more time if we are to be for ever with him
and with his Lord in Paradise. Let all old and
fast-dying men have this written up, like Augustine, on the wall over against their bed—"There is
life in a look at the crucified One." For we may
not have time nor strength for more than just one
such look of despatch.

And, then, if you would see the most wonderful
believer this world has ever seen, come to the cross
of Christ, and to that cross beside it, and look at
the penitent thief. He was a greater believer than
Abraham, the father of believers. Greater than
David. Greater than Isaiah. While Peter, and
James, and John, with all their privileges and
opportunities, are not worthy to be named in the
same day with this thief. For they had all forsaken their Saviour that awful day and had fled
from Him. It was of the thief, and of his alone
and so transcendent faith, that our Lord spoke in
such praise and in such reproof to Thomas eight
days afterwards, and said, 'Blessed is he in heaven
with Me this day, who saw nothing but shame, and
defeat, and death in Me, and yet so believed in Me,
and so cheered Me that day.' For our Lord never,
all His life, got such a surprise and such a delight
as He got on the cross that day,—not from Peter,
not from the Syrophœnician woman, not from the
centurion, not from Mary Magdalene, as He got
on His cross that morning from the thief who hung
beside Him. There was nothing, after His Father's
presence with Him, that held our Lord's heart
up all His life on earth like faith on Him in

any sinner's heart. And now that His Father also has forsaken Him; now that He is so absolutely deserted and so awfully alone; it is this thief's faith, and love, and hope that is such a cup of cold water to our Lord's fast-sinking heart. All faith and all hope on Christ were as dead as a stone in Peter's heart and in John's heart. Mary Magdalene herself, with all her love, had given Him up as for ever dead. But not the thief. It was at the very darkest hour this world has ever seen, or ever will see, that this thief's splendid faith flashed up brighter than the mid-day sun that day. Some say that Paul will sit next to Christ in Paradise. I cannot but think that Paul will insist on giving place to this very prince and leader of all New Testament believers. Anybody could have believed and laboured all their days after being caught up into the third heaven, and after seeing Christ sitting there in all His glory. But Christ was still on His cross, and His glory was as black as midnight, when all the faith of the church of God found its last retreat and sure fast-ness and high tower in the thief's unconquerable and inextinguishable heart. Paul deserves a high seat in heaven, and he will get all that he deserves, and more. But the penitent thief could say, "I am crucified with Christ" in a sense that even Paul could not say that. And however high the thief's throne in heaven is, the whole church of angels and saints will acclaim that he is worthy. Well done! O greatest and bravest-hearted of all be-lievers! Well done!

LXXXVIII

THOMAS

HE character of Thomas is an anatomy of melancholy. If "to say man is to say melancholy," then to say Thomas, called Didymus, is to say religious melancholy. Peter was of such an ardent and enthusiastical temperament that he was always speaking, whereas Thomas was too great a melancholian to speak much, and when he ever did speak it was always out of the depths of his hypochondriacal heart.

It was already the last week of his Master's life before we have Thomas so much as once opening his mouth. And the occasion of his first melancholy utterance was this : Lazarus was sick unto death in Bethany. And when Jesus heard that His friend was so sick, He said to His disciples, "Let us go into Judea again." "Master," they answered, "the Jews of late have been seeking opportunity to stone Thee to death, and goest Thou thither again?" And it was when Thomas saw that his Master was walking straight into the jaws of certain destruction that he said, in sad abandonment of all his remaining hope, "Let us also go, that we may die with Him." Thomas felt sure in his foreboding heart that his Master would never leave Judea alive; Thomas loved his Master more than life, and therefore he determined to die with Him. And, indeed, that determination was not very difficult for Thomas to take. Life had not yielded much to Thomas. And its best promises, more and more delayed, and more and more deluding him, were taking less and less hold of Thomas's heart as the years went on. We see now that the disciples of Jesus of Nazareth had the very best cause for high hope and full assurance. But at that time, and especially that week, Thomas had only too good ground for all his anxiety, and despondency, and melancholy. And a whole lifetime of melancholy, constitutional and circumstantial, had by this time settled down on Thomas, and had taken absolute and tyrannical possession of him. The disciples were all sick at heart with hope deferred; as also with the terrible questionings that would sometimes arise in their hearts, and would not be silenced; all kinds of questionings about their more and more mysterious Master; and about His more and more mysterious, and more and more stumbling, sayings, both about Himself and about themselves. And then His certainly impending death, and the unaccountable delay and disappearance of His promised kingdom: all that doubt, and fear, and despondency, and despair, met in Thomas's melancholy heart till it all took absolute possession of him. And till he sometimes said to himself that it would be the best thing that could happen to him if he could but die at once and be done for ever with all these difficulties and delays and bitter and unbearable disappointments. The discipleship-life, at its very best, had never been very satisfying to Thomas's heart; and, of late, it had been becoming absolutely unbearable to this melancholy and morose man. "Let us go," he said, "that we may die with Him."

The next time that Thomas speaks is when Jesus and His disciples are still in the upper room where the last passover had just been celebrated and the Lord's Supper instituted. "In My Father's house are many mansions: I go to prepare a place for you. And whither I go ye know, and the way ye know." The other disciples may know whither their Master is going, and they may know the way, but Thomas knows neither. The other disciples, as a matter of fact, know quite as little, and even less, about this whole matter than Thomas knows: only they think they know, when they do not: they have not knowledge enough to know that they know nothing. 'His Father's house?' said Thomas to himself. 'What does He mean? Why does He not speak plaiuly?' Thomas must understand his Master's meaning. Thomas is one of those unhappy men who cannot be put off with mere words. Thomas must see to the bottom before he can pretend to believe. Thomas was the first of those disciples, and a primate among them, in whose restless minds

> doubt,
> Like a shoot, springs round the stock of truth.

At the same time, Thomas in his melancholy candour and saddened plainness of speech was but ministering an opportunity to his Master to utter one of His most golden oracles. Jesus saith unto Thomas, "I am the way, the truth, and the life: no man cometh unto the Father but by Me." We cannot much regret that restless and realistic melancholy of Thomas since it has procured for us such a satisfying and ennobling utterance as that. "All His disciples minister to Him," says Newman; "and as in other ways, so also in giving occasion for the words of grace which proceed from His mouth."

Ten days pass. But what days! The betrayal, the arrest, the trial, the crucifixion, the burial, and the resurrection of Thomas's Master. What days and nights of trial, and that not for faith and hope only, but for reason herself to keep her seat! All the faith and all the trust of the disciples have not only fallen into a deep doubt during those terrible days and nights: all their faith and all their trust have been actually crucified and laid dead and buried, and that without a spark of hope. For as yet the disciples knew not the Scripture, that their Master must rise again from the dead. "Then the same day at evening, being the first day of the week, came Jesus and stood in the midst, and saith unto them, Peace be unto you. And when He had so said, He showed them His hands and His side. Then were the disciples glad when they saw the Lord." But Thomas was not with them when Jesus came. Where was Thomas that glorious Sabbath

evening? Why was he not with the rest? How
shall we account for the absence of Thomas? It
could not have been by accident. He must have
been told that the ten astounded, overwhelmed, and
enraptured disciples were to be all together that
wonderful night; astounded, overwhelmed, and
enraptured with the events of the morning. What
conceivable cause, then, could have kept Thomas
away? Whatever it was that kept Thomas away,
he was terribly punished for his absence. For he
thereby lost the first and best sight of his risen
Master, and His first and best benediction of peace.
He not only lost that benediction, but the joy of
the other disciples who had received it filled the
cup of Thomas's misery full. The first appearance
of their risen Master, that had lifted all the other
disciples up to heaven, was the last blow to cast
Thomas down to hell. The darkness, the bitterness, the sullenness, the pride, that had its seat so
deep down in Thomas's heart, all burst out in the
presence of his brethren's joy. Thomas would have
none of their joy. Thomas would not believe it.
They were dreaming. They were deluded. They
were mad. And the pride, and jealousy, and bitterness of his heart, all drove Thomas into a deeper rage
and a deeper rebellion. "Except I shall see in His
hands the print of the nails, and put my finger
into the print of the nails, and thrust my hand into
His side, I will not believe." We all understand
Thomas's misery. We have all been possessed by
it. It is the jealousy and the rage of a guilty
conscience. It is the jealousy and the rage of a

disappointed and a revengeful heart. When any
good comes to others that we should have been
sharers in, when we are absent through our own
fault, and when those who were present come to
tell us about all that we have lost, we have all
been like Thomas. We said, I do not believe it.
It was not all that you say it was. You are exalt-
ing yourselves over me. You are boasting yourselves beyond the truth. And if the truth cannot
be hid from us, or denied by us, we hate them, and
the thing we have lost, all the more. Thomas is
told us for our learning. We see ourselves in
Thomas as in a glass. Thomas, in all his melancholy and resentment, is ourselves. Unbelief, and
obstinacy, and loss of opportunity, and then increased unbelief, is no strange thing to ourselves.

And after eight days the disciples were again
within, and this time Thomas was with them. It
had taken the disciples all their might all these
eight days to prevail with and to persuade Thomas.
And all of us who know what it is to wage a war
with our own wounded pride, and with nothing but
our own sullenness, and stubbornness, and mulish-
ness to oppose to the pleadings of truth and love,
we know something of what Thomas came through
before he consented to accompany the other disciples
to the upper room at the end of those eight days.
"Then came Jesus, the doors being shut, and stood
in the midst, and said, Peace be unto you. Then
saith He to Thomas, Reach hither thy finger, and
behold My hands; and reach hither thy hand and
thrust it into My side, and be not faithless but

believing." How Thomas would hate himself when his own scornful, unbelieving, contemptuous words came back to him from his Master's gracious lips! How utterly odious his own words would sound as his Master repeated them. And worst of all when his risen Master humbled Himself to meet Thomas's unbelieving words and to satisfy them! Thomas would have killed himself with shame and self-condemnation, had it not been given him at that grandest moment of his whole life to say, "My Lord and my God!" Jesus saith unto him, "Thomas, because thou hast seen Me, thou hast believed; blessed are they that have not seen, and yet have believed!"

Now, my brethren, do you clearly understand and accept this peculiar blessedness of believing without seeing? Do you clearly see and fully accept the blessedness of a strong and an easy acting faith in the things of Christ? Faith is always easy where love and hope are strong. What we live for and hope to see, what we love with our whole heart, what we pray for night and day, what our whole future is anchored upon, that we easily believe, that we are ready to welcome. In that case our faith is to us nothing less than the substance of the thing hoped for; it is the evidence of the thing not seen as yet. What with Thomas's temperament of melancholy; what with his not having hid in his heart the things that our Lord had so often said about His coming death for sin and His resurrection for salvation; and then his hot jealousy and ill-will at the joyful news of the disciples; with all that Thomas's heart was in a state most deadly to faith. Had Thomas's heart been tender, had he had seven devils cast out of his heart like Mary Magdalene, he also would have gone out to the sepulchre while it was yet dark, and would have been the first of all the disciples to see his risen Lord. But, as it was, he was the last to see Him, and ran a close risk of never seeing Him in this world. Now, how is it with you in this same matter? Are you hard to convince? Are you slow of faith? Is your heart so set upon this world that you have no eyes or ears for the world to come? Are you able to dispense with Jesus Christ day after day till He dies out of your heart, and imagination, and whole life, altogether? Unbelief grows by what it feeds upon, just like faith and love. To him who has no faith in God, in Christ, in the Holy Scriptures, in the unseen world, and in the world to come, from him is even taken away the little faith that he had, till he has none at all. You know men in whom that awful catastrophe has taken place. You know it, in measure, in yourself. Your faith is all but dead. You do not wait for Christ's coming, either to judge the world, or to take you to Himself, or to sanctify you, and comfort you, and answer your prayers. And then you are uneasy, and unhappy, and jealous, and angry, when you hear that He has been manifesting Himself in all these ways to them that believe. But you were not waiting for Him. You neither expected Him nor wished for Him: and He never comes to the like of you till He comes at last and too late. You will be horrified when it is told you what your whole life, and your whole heart, and all your desires

"Blessed are they that have not seen, and yet have believed."

and hopes say when words are put upon them. They
all say, ' I will not believe till the last trump awakens
me, and the graves are opened, and the great white
throne is set.'

Now, from Thomas and his Lord that night let
us learn this also, and take it away. Let us act upon
the faith we have. Let us frequent the places where
He is said to manifest Himself. Let us feed our
faith on the strong meat of His word. And, since
here also acts produce habits, and habits character;
let us act faith continually on faith's great objects
and operations. And, especially, on our glorified
Redeemer. To Thomas He was crucified yesterday.
But to us He is risen, and exalted, and is soon to
come again. That the trial of your faith, being
much more precious than of gold that perisheth,
might be found unto praise, and honour, and glory
at the appearing of Jesus Christ. Whom having
not seen, ye love: in whom, though now ye see Him
not, yet believing, ye rejoice with joy unspeakable
and full of glory.

> For all thy rankling doubts so sore,
>   Love thou thy Saviour still,
> Him for thy Lord and God adore,
>   And ever do His will.
> Though vexing thoughts may seem to last,
> Let not thy soul be quite o'ercast;
> Soon will He show thee all His wounds and say,
> Long have I known thy name: know thou My face alway

LXXXIX

CLEOPAS AND HIS COMPANION

LEOPAS and his companion were two
men of Emmaus who had gone up the
week before to Jerusalem to keep the
passover. Cleopas and his companion
were not exactly disciples of our Lord.
That is to say, their names were not among the
twelve ; though the likelihood is that they were
numbered and were well known among the seventy.
And they had gone up to the feast in the hope that
their Lord would be there, and that they would both
see and hear Him as on former feast-days. It seemed
to them like a year, like a lifetime, like another
world, since last week they walked and talked together so full of hope and expectation, all the way
up from Emmaus to Jerusalem. For Jesus had
come up to the passover, as they had expected He
would. And they had both seen Him, and had
heard Him speak. They had followed Him about
in the streets of Jerusalem as He preached His last
sermons, so terrible to them to see and to hear.
They were not among the twelve, and they had not
been invited to the upper room, but they had done
the next best thing to that, for they had eaten their

passover supper out at Bethany with their friend
Lazarus, and with Martha and Mary his sisters.
The whole of Bethany was absolutely overwhelmed
when the news came out at midnight that Jesus had
been betrayed by one of His disciples, and was at
that moment in the hands of His enemies. And
with their loins girt, and with their passover-staff
in their hands, Lazarus, and Cleopas, and his companion, were abroad in the streets of Jerusalem all
that night, and till after the crucifixion was finished
next morning. And now the third day of that
tremendous overthrow and shipwreck had come,
when, with a sickness of heart indescribable, Cleopas
at last said to his companion, 'Rise, and let us
shake the dust off our feet against this accursed city,
and let us escape to our own home.' True; certain
women of their company had rushed into the city
that morning, saying that they had seen a vision of
angels who told them that their crucified Master had
risen and left His grave; but to Cleopas all that
was so many idle tales. 'No, no!' Cleopas said to
his companion, 'come away home. Believe me, we
have seen the last of the redemption of Israel in our
day, at any rate.' Why, you will ask, was Cleopas
in such a hurry to get home? Might he not have
gone out to see the empty grave for himself? Might
he not have waited in Jerusalem till the end of
"the third day" that his Master so often foretold
about Himself? As it was, Cleopas, like Pliable in
the *Pilgrim's Progress*, was making a desperate
plunge through the Slough of Despond so as to get
out on the side next his own house, when a man

M

whose name was Help came and held out His hand to
him, and to his companion, in the midst of the Slough.

Yes: Cleopas and his companion, like Mr. Fear-
ing, had a perfect Slough of Despond in their own
hearts that sunset as they walked down to Emmaus
and reasoned together and were sad. 'Where did
you see Him first? What was it that led you to
think that He was the Christ? And, did you hear
this sermon, and that? And this parable and that?'
And then the arrest, and the trial, and the crucifixion. No wonder they reeled to and fro, and
staggered under their load of sorrow, till the
workers in the fields said they were two drunken
men on their way home from the feast. When a
stranger overtook them as they halted, and reasoned,
and debated together in their sadness. 'Peace be
with you both!' said the stranger with a pleasant
voice as he joined himself to their company. But
Cleopas was scarcely civil. Cleopas scarcely returned
the salute of the stranger, so overwhelmed was he
with his sadness. And they walked on in silence,
Cleopas and his companion, and the stranger. Till
the sympathising stranger broke the sad silence
with these confiding words: " What manner of com-
munications are these that ye have one to another,
as ye walk and are sad?" 'Art thou such a stranger
in Jerusalem,' answered Cleopas, 'as not to know the
things which are come to pass there in these days?
Where wert thou all last week? Where wert thou
last Friday? Thou canst not have been in Jerusalem, surely, for all Jerusalem was out at Calvary
that morning. And if thou hadst been out there

thou wouldst not wonder at our sadness.' The
stranger did not say whether he had been out at
Calvary last Friday morning or no. "What things?"
He asked, bowing, at it were, to Cleopas's reproof
and reproach at such unaccountable ignorance at
such a time. And then we have Cleopas's reply in
his own very identical words. For Luke, you must
know, when he was preparing himself for his Gospel,
and when he had read Mark's meagre verses about
the Emmaus meeting, said to himself, 'I must be at
the bottom of this! I must have a much fuller
record of all this in my Gospel. I wonder if Cleopas is still alive?' And thus it is that we have
before us, *verbatim et literatim*, the exact answer
that Cleopas gave to the stranger when he asked,
"What things?" 'I remember, as if it were but
yesterday,' said Cleopas to Luke, 'the whole scene,
and every word that He said to us, and that we said
to Him. How could I ever forget a single syllable
of it? It was all so burned into my heart that I
have told it a thousand times.' And Cleopas took
the Evangelist out of Emmaus and showed him the
very spot just where the stranger joined them, and
just where He said, "What things?" 'And just
where I said—these were my very words to Him—
I said, Concerning Jesus of Nazareth, which was a
prophet mighty in deed and in word before God
and all the people. And how the chief priests and
our rulers delivered Him to be condemned to death,
and have crucified Him. But we trusted, I went
on in my folly, that it had been He who should
have redeemed Israel: and beside all this, to-day is

the third day since these things were done. And
from that hour to this, I have never for an hour or
may say never for a moment, forgotten the look He
gave us when He said to us, "O fools, and slow of
heart to believe!"' And then Cleopas continued
to relate to Luke the rest of that never-to-be-
forgotten conversation concerning the true Christ in
Moses and the prophets. What an hour that was
to Cleopas and to his companion! They did not
know where they were. They forgot themselves.
They were carried captive with the stranger's amazing knowledge, and with His supreme authority,
and with His burning words. And no wonder.
Many learned, and earnest, and eloquent men have
expounded Moses, and David, and Isaiah since that
Emmaus afternoon; but human ears and human
hearts have never heard such another exposition of
Holy Scripture as Cleopas and his companion heard
at that stranger's lips. For, this was an Interpreter,
one among a thousand! When this Interpreter
gave His first interpretation of Scripture in Nazareth
three years before, there was delivered to Him the
book of the prophet Isaiah. But they had no book
to deliver Him on the way to Emmaus. Nor did He
need a book. This stranger, whoever He was, seemed
to Cleopas to have the whole book unrolled within
Himself. He seemed to have Moses, and David,
and Isaiah, and Jeremiah, absolutely by heart. And
the way He spake to them called to His two companions' remembrance all that they had ever heard
or read in Moses, and the Prophets, and the Psalms.
The seed of the woman; the brazen serpent; the

paschal lamb; the scapegoat; the thirty pieces of
silver. My God, my God, why hast thou forsaken
me? They part my garments among them, and cast
lots upon my vesture. Reproach hath broken mine
heart: I looked for some to take pity, but there was
none: and for comforters, but I found none. They
gave me also gall for my meat, and in my thirst
they gave me vinegar to drink. He was wounded for
our transgressions, He was bruised for our iniquities;
the chastisement of our peace was upon Him: and
with His stripes we are healed. He is brought as
a lamb to the slaughter, and as a sheep before her
shearers is dumb, so He opened not His mouth.
'O, fool that I was!' Cleopas cried out to Luke.
'I had seen it all fulfilled the week before with mine
own eyes. But, that evening, our eyes were somehow holden that we did not know Him again! At
the same time how our hearts did burn as He spake
these things to us. And then He said to us, appealing to us to reply: May not Jesus of Nazareth be
the true Christ of God, and your own Redeemer
after all? After all, may not Jesus of Nazareth
be He who was to come? Do not all your own
prophets tell you that the true Christ must be
denied of His own, and delivered up to Pilate to
crucify? Must not the Prince of Life, when He
comes, be killed and raised from the dead on the
third day? What think ye? What say ye? And
have you not just told me yourselves that certain
women of your own company were early this very
morning at the sepulchre, and that the angels of
heaven were descended there to testify that Jesus

of Nazareth was alive again ?' And so on, till their
hearts burned within them like two coals of juniper.

O ye men still of Emmaus, now sitting and hearing
all that in this house! I implore you to open your
heart also to your Lord's burning words about
Himself. To speak plainly, I implore you to seek
out in this city that expounder, that one of a
thousand preachers, who makes your heart to burn.
If by chance, so to call it, you enter a church in
this city of churches on a Sabbath day, with your
heart sad, with your hopes ashamed, with your expectations a complete shipwreck, like Cleopas and
his desponding companion, and the preacher so
opens God's word to you, so sets forth the redemption of Israel and your own redemption, so
sets forth a suffering Redeemer and His suffering
people, that your heart is in a flame all that day,
then, that is the preacher in all this world for you.
That is my servant for you, says your God to
you. I have made his mouth like a sharp sword
for you. I have made him a polished shaft for
you. I have hid him in my quiver for you. Hear
him, said the Father, concerning his preacher-Son.
And that preacher you have just heard may be as
great a stranger to you as our Lord was to Cleopas
on that highway that afternoon; but, if I were
you, I would find out his name, and where God
has given him his pulpit. If I were you I would
have him for my minister, and for my children's
minister, at any cost. I would sell my present house
and buy another to be near that preacher. And
if you never hear such a preacher; if no preacher

has ever made your heart to burn; if there is not
in all the city a single heart-kindling, heart-com-
manding, heart-capturing preacher for you, then, at
any rate, there are not a few heart-kindling and
heart-holding authors to be had.   Authors, thanks
be to God, that will make you all but independent
of us lukewarm preachers.   Do you know some of
those authors' names?   Do any of you almost owe
your soul to some of them?   Do you have a select
shelf of them within reach of your chair and your
bed?   Could you say, if not of some spiritual
preacher, then of some spiritual writer, what Crashaw
says of Teresa: "The flame 1 took from reading
thee."   And what Cleopas said to Luke about this
stranger's words, "Did not our heart burn within
us?"   I preached sin with great sense, says John
Bunyan.   And I warrant you that stranger preached
the Messianic and the Atonement passages in David,
and in Isaiah, and in Jeremiah, and in Zechariah,
with great sense also, and for a very good reason.

> Yea, this man's brow, like to a title-leaf,
> Foretells the nature of a tragic volume:
> He trembles, and the whiteness in his cheek
> Is apter than his tongue to tell his errand.

Never did threescore furlongs seem so short since
furlongs were laid out on the face of the earth.
'Come and sup with us,' said the entranced Cleopas
to this mysterious stranger who had so over-mastered
him, and so set his heart on fire.   "Abide with
us, for the day is far spent."   And when they had
sat down to supper, Cleopas naturally asked the
stranger, as you would have done, to say grace.

What grace did that stranger say in that supper-room in Emmaus, I wonder? John Livingstone tells us that John Smith of Maxtown in Teviot-dale had all the Psalms of David by heart, and that, instead of our curt and grudging grace before meat he always repeated to his attentive table a whole Psalm. Would it be at Emmaus the twenty-third Psalm. Would it be the twenty-seventh and the twenty-eighth verses of the hundred and fourth Psalm? Or, would it be Job's every Sabbath morning and every Sabbath evening grace and bless-ing? Or, would it be something that the stranger made up on the spot? Would it be this, at the hearing of which Cleopas's heart would kindle again? "Except ye eat the flesh of the Son of Man, and drink His blood, ye have no life in you. For My flesh is meat indeed, and My blood is drink indeed." Whatever the grace was that He said, you may be quite sure He did not say it as we say our graces. He did not mumble it over so that nobody could hear it. He did not say it as if He was ashamed of it. He did not say, Amen! with His hand down already in the dish. Neither did Cleopas and his companion sit down and begin to eat before the grace was finished. No! for the truth is, the three men got no further than the grace that night. That sacred supper, with such a grace said over it, stands on that table to this day. It is not eaten to this day. For as the stranger handed to Cleopas and to his companion the bread He had blessed and broken, they could not but see His Hands! And the moment they saw His Hands, He had vanished out of their sight.

XC

MATTHIAS THE SUCCESSOR TO JUDAS ISCARIOT

IN the opening chapter of the Acts of the Apostles we are introduced into the first congregational meeting, so to call it, that ever was held in the Church of Christ. There are a hundred-and-twenty members present in the upper room, and the Presbytery of Jerusalem are met there with the congregation: moderator, clerk, and all. Peter presides; and he discharges the duties of the day with all that solemnity of mind and all that intensity of heart which we seldom miss in Peter. The solemnity of the meeting would solemnise any man. It would melt a far harder heart than the heart of the emotional son of Jonas ever was. For Judas Iscariot, a member of the Presbytery, so to call him, has turned out to have been the son of perdition all the time. For thirty pieces of silver he had become guide to them that took Jesus. Peter himself had wellnigh gone down into the same horrible pit with Judas: and he also would have been in his own place by this time, had it not been that his Master prayed for Peter that his faith might not fail. And thus it is that Peter is now sitting in that seat of honour and influence and authority, and is conducting the election of a successor to Judas, with all that holy fear and with all that firm faith which makes that upper room, under Peter's presidency, such a pattern to all vacant congregations to all time. Considering her age and her size, the Church of Jerusalem had a large number of men any one of whom could quite well have been put forward and proposed for the vacant office. But Peter and his colleagues, with a great sense of responsibility, had prepared a short leet of two quite outstanding and distinguished men; Joseph, who was surnamed Justus, and Matthias. And then one of the eleven led the congregation in prayer in these well-remembered words—"Lord, Thou knowest the hearts of all men: show whether of these two Thou hast chosen." And the lot fell upon Matthias, and he was numbered with the eleven apostles.

Now, somewhat remarkable to say, never before the day of his election, and never after it, is Matthias's name so much as once mentioned in all the New Testament. At the same time, we have Matthias's footprints, so to speak, oftener than once on the pages of the four Gospels. And a man's mere footprints, and the direction they point to, will sometimes tell us far more about the real character and capacity of the man than whole volumes of printed matter about him. The first time we see one of Matthias's footprints is on the sands of Bethabara beyond Jordan, where John was baptizing. Like Andrew and Simon the sons of Jonas, and like John the son of Zebedee, Matthias

was a disciple of the Baptist at that time, confessing his sins.   The next day John seeth Jesus
coming to him, and saith to Matthias, Behold the
Lamb of God.   And Matthias heard him speak, and
he followed Jesus, along with John and Andrew.
And when Peter tabled Matthias's name on the
day of the election, he certified all these things
about Matthias to the ten, and to the women, and
to Mary the mother of Jesus, and to His brethren,
and to the whole hundred-and-twenty.   And more
than that, Peter certified to the whole congregation that, when many who had been baptized,
apostatised and went back and walked no more
with John and Jesus, Matthias, said Peter, has
this to his praise, that he has endured and has
persevered up to this very present.   Not only so,
but this also, that Matthias had been a witness
with the eleven of the resurrection of the Lord.
And these, added Peter, are the two indispensable
tests of fitness for this vacant office ; a three years'
conversion and faithful discipleship, and this also,
that he had seen the risen Lord with his own eyes.
And the lot fell upon Matthias.

Now, it is sometimes not very unlike that when
you yourselves meet to call a minister. Tremendous
as the moment is : everlasting as the issues are that
hang upon that moment : you may never have
heard so much as the name of that candidate for
the pastorate of your immortal soul.   You may
never so much as have heard him once open his
mouth either to pray or to preach.   Not one of the
hundred-and-twenty had ever heard this stranger

man Matthias once open his mouth. But Peter has
had his eye on Matthias all along. Peter knew far
more about both Joseph and Matthias than they
could have believed. Peter was all ears and all eyes
where a future apostle and pastor was concerned.
And so it is sometimes still. All you really know
about your future minister you have to take sometimes on the best testimony you can get. As one of
our own elders once said when we were calling our
young minister: " I would rather trust to those two
capable men who know him and have heard him
preach, than I would trust to my own ears." And
he spake with both wisdom and humility in so saying. Like the hundred-and-twenty, little as you
know about your future minister, you know this
much, that when all the other young men at school
and college were choosing learning, and philosophy,
and medicine, and law, and the army, and the navy,
and trade, and manufactures, and so on; this youth
now in your offer was led to choose the word of
God, and the pulpit, and the pastorate, for his life-
work. And, with all that, you may with some
assurance, put your hand to his call, after you have
made your importunate and personal prayer about
this whole momentous matter to Him who knows
the hearts of all men. For He knows your heart
better than you know it yourself: and He knows
just what kind of a minister your heart needs: your
own heart and your children's hearts. And, then,
He knows the hearts of all those probationers also,
and whether their hearts are properly in their
Master's work or no. As also what motive it was

that made them ministers at first, and with what
motive and with what intention they are laying out
their future work among you. How well it is, both
for congregations and candidates, that He knows all
men's hearts, and that all men's hearts are in His
hands.

Three years ago Matthias had come through a
very sharp trial of faith, and love, and patience,
and perseverance. At his conversion and baptism
Matthias had prepared his heart to leave all and to
follow Christ. But instead of being invited to do
what with all his heart he wished to do, Matthias
was deliberately passed over by our Lord in His
election of the twelve. Matthias had been in Christ,
as Paul says, a long time before some of those men
who were lifted over his head; and here was he as
good as set aside and clean forgotten. And, just
suppose, what is more than likely, that Matthias
knew Judas's secret heart and real character quite
well; what a shock it was to Matthias's faith, and
love, and whole religious life, to see such a deceiver
as Iscariot was, deliberately chosen by Christ, when
Matthias would have shed the last drop of his blood
for the Master who had refused to employ him.
But Matthias, for all that, did not let his heart
sour. He accepted being set aside as his proper
place. He found in himself only too many reasons
why he was so set aside. He was like the defeated
candidate in Plutarch who, departing home from the
election to his house, said to them at home that
it did him good to see that there were three hundred men in Athens who were better men than he

was. And thus it was that when many men would
have turned away and gone after another master,
Matthias said to himself : ' Office or no office,
election or rejection, call or no call, to whom else
can I go ? ' Nay, not only did Matthias keep true
to his Master through all these humiliations and
disappointments, but he continued to behave himself and to lay out his life just as if he had been
elected and ordained. So much so, that without
ordination he worked harder at the out-of-the-way
work of the discipleship than some of those did who
were elected, and ordained, and honoured, and
rewarded men. And thus it was that Peter was
able to certify to the hundred-and-twenty that
Matthias had been as true and as loyal to his Lord
all those three years as the very best of the eleven
had been. ' And thus,' said Peter, ' if there were
some who were numbered among us who were not
at heart of us, there were others who were at heart
and in life really of us, though they were not as yet
written down among us.' So have I myself seen
heaven-born and highly-gifted ministers of Christ
passed over in the day when this and that vacant
charge met to cast their lots. And, like Matthias,
I have seen such men left out at the beginning
only to be the more promoted and employed in the
end. But then, to be sure, they were like Matthias
in this also, that all their days they were men of
staunchest loyalty to their Master, and men of
sleepless labour for His cause. When a door shall
open, and where, is not the true servant's business,
nor his anxiety. It is the true servant's part to be

ready; which the truest of all servants never feels
that he is. And disappointments and procrastina-
tions to all such men are but extended opportunities
to enable them to be somewhat less unready for
their call when it comes. If Matthias had been a
modern probationer you would not have found him
going about complaining against this committee
and that congregation. You would not have seen
him going about idle all the week, and then turning up at each new vacancy with the same old and
oft-fingered sermon. No. You may shut all your
doors on some candidates, but you cannot shut
them out from their books, and from the hidden
and unstipended work that their hearts love. You
cannot, with all your ill-cast lots, either embitter
or alienate a truly elect, and humble-minded, and
diligent disciple of Christ. And with all your ill-
advised elections the stone that is fit for the wall
will not always be let lie in the ditch.

But is there anything possible to our very best
probationers that can at all be compared to this
qualification of those days—to have companied with
the Lord Jesus all the time He went out and in
among His disciples? Yes; I think there is. Nay,
not only so; but when we enter into all the in-
wardness and depth of this matter we come to see
that our students of divinity and our probationers
have actually some great advantages over the twelve
disciples themselves. Our Lord's words are final,
and full of instruction and comfort to us, on this
matter. His words to Thomas, I mean. Jesus
saith to him "Thomas, because thou hast seen,

thou hast believed; blessed are they that have not
seen, and yet have believed." And you will all
recall Sir Thomas Browne's noble protestation:
"Now, honestly, I bless myself that I never saw
Christ nor His disciples. I would not have been
one of Christ's patients on whom He wrought His
wonders. For then had my faith been thrust upon
me, nor should I enjoy that greater blessing pronounced to all that believe and saw not. I believe
He was dead and buried, and rose again: and desire
to see Him in His glory, rather than to contem-
plate Him in His cenotaph or sepulchre. They
only had the advantage of a bold and noble faith
who lived before His coming, and who upon obscure
prophecies and mystical types could raise a belief
and expect apparent impossibilities." To have seen
and handled the Word of Life; to have had Him
dwelling among them, full of grace and truth, as
John says; to have had Him going in and out
among them, as Peter says, was a privilege incomparable and unspeakable. At the same time, let
any student in our day read his Greek Testament,
with his eye on the Object: let him be like John
Bunyan:—"Methought I was as if I had seen Him
born, as if I had seen Him grow up, as if I had
seen Him walk through this world, from the Cradle
to the Cross: to which, when He came, I saw how
gently He gave Himself up to be hanged and nailed
on it for my sins and wicked doings. Also, as I
was musing on this His progress, that dropped on
my spirit, He was ordained for the slaughter," and
so on. Let any of our students company with
Christ all the time He went in and out in that

manner, and he may depend upon it that the
beautiful benediction which our Lord addressed in
reproof to Thomas will be richly fulfilled to that
wise-hearted student all his happy ministerial days,
and through him to his happy people. Now, if
there were a divinity student here I would ask and
demand of him out of this Scripture for students—
Are you so companying with Christ while you are
still at college? Do you see with all your inward
eyes what you read in your New Testament? Do
you believe and believe and believe your way through
the four Gospels? Is your faith the very substance
itself of the things you hope for, and the absolute
and conclusive evidence of the things you do not as
yet see? Do you pray your way through the life
of Christ? Do you put the lepers, and the sick,
and the possessed with devils, and the dead in their
graves, out of their places, as you read about them;
and do you put yourself into their places, and say
what they say, and hear and accept what is said to
them? For, if so, then you will receive, all your
preaching and pastoral days, the end of your faith,
the salvation of your own soul, and the salvation of
the souls of your people.

Then, again, could any of our probationers be
put forward by his proposer as Matthias was still
put forward by Peter? No. It could not possibly
be said of any man living in these dregs of time of
ours that he had been an actual witness of the resurrection of Christ. And yet I am not so sure of that.
Strange things can be said when you come to speak
about a true probationer. With man it is impossible; but not with God With God all things are

N

possible. I myself know probationers who are witnesses of the very best authority that Christ is risen indeed. Let such a young preacher come to your vacant pulpit with Ephesians i. 19 to ii. 1 for his Sabbath morning exposition; and let him set forth with Paul, that the spiritual quickening of a soul dead in trespasses and sins is done by the same mighty power that quickened and raised up Christ, and you will soon see if he knows what he is speaking about. And if he does: if he makes your hearts to burn with the noble doctrine of his and your oneness with the risen Christ, then you have in your offer a living witness of apostolic rank for Christ's resurrection. You might have the angel who rolled away the stone and sat on it for your other candidate, but he should have no vote of mine. Give me for my minister, not Gabriel himself, but a fellow-sinner who has been quickened together with Christ, and who can describe the process and the experience till my death-cold heart burns within me with the resurrection-life of Christ. Give me a minister whom God has raised from the dead, and you may have all the sounding brasses and tinkling cymbals in heaven and earth for me. And I am glad to say that there are not a few probationers abroad of that experience. Only, are you sure you will recognise them when they appear and preach in your pulpit? For—

A jest's prosperity lies in the ear
Of him that hears it, never in the tongue
Of him that speaks it.

Let the hundred-and-twenty take heed how they hear.

XCI

ANANIAS AND SAPPHIRA

THEMISTOCLES tossed all night and could not sleep because of the laurels of Miltiades. And Ananias was like Themistocles because of the praises poured upon Barnabas by Peter, and by all the apostles, and by all the poor. Ananias and Sapphira could not take rest till they, like Barnabas, had sold their possession, and laid the price of it at Peter's feet. 'Lay it at Peter's feet,' said Sapphira to her hesitating husband, 'and say that you are very sorry that the land did not sell for far more. And after I have made my purchases, I will come to the Lord's Supper with you. Keep a place for me at the Table, and I will join you there in good time in breaking of bread and in prayers.' And Ananias did as Sapphira had instigated him to do. Only, Ananias was not at all happy in his approach to Peter's feet that day. Somehow or other, Ananias could not summon up that gladness and that singleness of heart with which all the other contributors came up that day. With all he could do there was a certain awkwardness and stumblingness of manner that

Ananias, somehow or other, could not shake off all that day. You who are collectors for churches and charities are well accustomed to all Ananias's looks and ways of speaking that day. You often hear from us the very same explanations and apologies and self-defences. 'There had been a great fall in the rent of land in Judea of late. And thus the old estate had not nearly yielded its upset and expected price. But what it had yielded, Peter was welcome to it.'

Everything fell to Peter in those days. The offices and services of the early Church had not as yet been divided up and specialised into the apostleship, and the eldership, and the deaconship, and, till that was done, Peter had to be everything himself. Peter was premier apostle, ruling elder, leading deacon, and all. It was like those country congregations where the minister has to do everything himself, till he has neither time nor strength nor spirit left to give himself continually to prayer, and to the ministry of the word. But Peter was a perfect Samson in the Israel of that day. He was a minister of immense capacity, gigantic energy, endless resource, and overpowering authority. And thus it was that it had fallen to Peter to sit over against the treasury, and to enter the Pentecostal contributions that day. And it struck Ananias like a thunderbolt, when Peter, instead of smiling upon him and praising him, denounced and sentenced him so sternly. " Ananias, why hath Satan filled thine heart to lie to the Holy Ghost?" And the young men arose, and wound him up, and carried him out, and buried him. And then, three hours after, just as Peter was shutting up his books to go to dispense the Lord's Supper, at that moment Sapphira appeared. 'You sold your farm for so much, your husband tells me?' 'Yes, my lord, for so much.' And the young men came in and found her dead, and they buried Ananias and Sapphira in Aceldama, next back-breadth to Judas Iscariot, the proprietor of the place. That the prophecy of Isaiah might be fulfilled: "They shall go forth, and look upon the carcases of the men that have transgressed against me; for their worm shall not die, neither shall their fire be quenched, and they shall be an abhorring unto all flesh." And that the prophecy of Daniel also might be fulfilled: "Many of them that sleep in the dust of the earth shall awake, some to everlasting life, and some to shame and everlasting contempt."

What a world this is we live in! What a red-hot furnace of sin and of sanctification is this world! How we all tempt and try and test and stumble one another in everything we say and do! Barnabas cannot sell his estate in Cyprus and lay the price of it at Peter's feet, but by doing so he must immediately become the sudden death of Ananias and Sapphira. But for the Pentecostal love, and but for Barnabas's baptism into that love, Ananias and Sapphira would have lived to see their children's children and peace upon Israel. They would have sat down together at the Lord's Table till Peter preached their funeral sermon and held them up as two pattern proprietors of houses and lands.

But Barnabas and his renowned name became such
a snare to Ananias and Sapphira that they were
buried on the same day and in the same grave.
Ama nesciri has been the motto of more than one
of the great saints. Seek obscurity, that is. Subscribe anonymously, that is. Do not let your
collectors and the advertising people print your
name or your amount, that is. Say, A Friend.
Say, A Well-wisher. Put a star, put a cross, put
anything but your name, not even your initials.
Or, if you are a popular author, say, and not a
landowner in these days; publish your books without your name. Employ another name. You may
miss something that is very sweet to you by doing
that; but it will be made up to you afterwards
when all your royalties come in, and all your last
day reviews. Think of Ananias and Sapphira when
all men praise your generosity, or your Shakesperian
genius, or your enormous emoluments. Be sure of
this, that all Peter's praises of Barnabas did not
refresh Barnabas's heart half so much as they
caused that sinful sleeplessness, and all its consequences, to Ananias and Sapphira.

"Satan hath filled thine heart, Ananias." That
was a terrible salutation for a man to be met with
who had just sold a possession and laid such a
large part of the price at the apostle's feet. But
Peter knew all Satan's processes. Peter knew by
experience what he was speaking about. And that is
the reason why Peter speaks with such assurance and
severity and indignation and judgment. And had
Ananias at that moment gone out and wept bitterly,

we would have been drawing far other lessons to-night out of that terrible Communion morning. Do you know the premonition, the sensation, the smell, so to say, when Satan approaches you to fill your heart? And what do you say to him? What do you do to him? Do you set a chair for him? Do you lay a cover and set glasses for him? Do you share your pillow with him? "Ah! you are there again, my man!" So an old saint in the congregation salutes Satan as often as her practised nostrils catch the beginning of his brimstone on her stairhead. "But you are too late this time. I am engaged to-day. There is Some One with me. And you had better flee at once. Come sooner next time!" Luther threw his ink-bottle. What do you throw? What do you do? Or is Satan in on you, and are you in his hands and at his service, in money matters, and what not, before you know where you are? " Ah, sir, you are there again, are you? But my heart is as full to-day as it can hold of Another," calls out my stairhead friend by reason of her exercised senses.

The stroke was sudden, and, as we say, severe. But even at this distance of time and place we can see some good and sufficient reasons for the severity of the stroke. *Pœna duorum doctrina multorum,* is the epigrammatic comment of an old writer. On two hands that sore stroke would tell for long. On the one hand, on those who were tempted to join the Christian community in order to share in the Pentecostal charity. For, then as now, a crowd of impostors would dog the steps of

the open-hearted and open-handed church.   On
the other hand, we all give very much as others
have given before us.   We measure our givings, not
by our duty nor by our ability, but by what others
have done, and by what is expected of us.   We wish
to impress you.   We wish to have your approval.
We say with Ananias: 'This is all I can spare;
indeed, this is all I possess.'   Our sin, and our
danger of death in our giving, lie not so much
in that we have given less than we could have
given, but in that we have not told the truth.
"Yea, for so much," we say, till the feet of the
young men are almost at our door.   The stroke
was sudden and severe to the onlookers, but it was
not at all so sudden or so severe to Ananias and
Sapphira themselves.   It was not so unexpected
and without warning to them.   There were many
provocations and aggravations on their part of
which we are quite ignorant.   Ananias may at
one time have been a poor man's son, and when
he came up to Jerusalem in his youth to push his
fortune, he may have knelt down on the side or
Olivet and said, 'Thy vows are upon me, O God.
And if Thou wilt give me bread to eat, and raiment
to put on, and a wife and children in Jerusalem,
then the Lord shall be my God, and the God of
my household.'   Or, again, in some time of adversity he may have said, "The pains of hell gat
hold upon me; but I will pay that which my mouth
spake when I was in trouble."   Or, again, in those
sweet but soul-deceiving days when they were bridegroom and bride together; in those Beulah days—

"As for me and my house, we will serve the Lord. Like David, we will walk with a perfect heart in all our household affairs at home." Ah, yes; God was no doubt quite sufficiently justified to Ananias and Sapphira themselves, when He judged them so swiftly that day. At the same time, Jeremy Taylor, who has given immense learning and intellect to all such cases, says that God sometimes accepts a temporal death in room of an eternal. And that, to some persons, a sudden death stands instead of a long and an explicit repentance. While Augustine, I see, and some other great authorities, are bold to class the awful case of Ananias and Sapphira under that scripture of the apostle where he assures us that some church members are delivered unto Satan for the destruction of the flesh, so that the spirit may be saved in the day of the Lord Jesus. Let us join with Augustine and Taylor in their burial-service over Ananias and Sapphira in the trembling hope that they were struck down in a sanctifying discipline, rather than in an everlasting condemnation. And that they so died that we might learn of them so to live as not to die. Let us hope that both husband and wife had the root of the matter in them all the time; and that we shall see them also saved in that day, in spite of Satan and all his fatal entrances into their hearts. The Lord rebuke thee, O Satan, is not this a brand plucked out of the fire?

And now to come home to ourselves. As you all know, we have an institution in full operation in the Free Church of Scotland which is based and built up and worked out on exactly Pentecostal and Barnabas principles. Dr. Chalmers's conception of the Sustentation Fund was derived and developed from the spirit and the example of the Apostolic Church of Jerusalem. The same Pentecostal spirit was poured out at the Disruption of the Established and Endowed Church of Scotland, to support the Free Church of Scotland under her injuries and her impoverishments for Christ's sake, and for the sake of His people. And thus it was that the ministers and deacons' courts of the Free Church were then, and are still, all of one mind and spirit, and have all things in common. And that same Pentecostal spirit breathes and burns, and that same Apostolic institution still stands and extends and expands, to this day. And still the Prophetic and Apostolic benediction is pronounced over the Free Church and her liberal-hearted people—" Bring ye all the tithes into the storehouse, saith the Lord of Hosts, and prove Me now herewith, if I will not open the windows of heaven, and pour you out a blessing, that there shall not be room enough to receive it."

" Prove Me now herewith," said the Lord. And He has promised that when we prove Him with our tithes,all manner of prosperity will follow our practice of that Scriptural rule and pattern. And the rule is not a Scriptural one only. Somehow or other, the tithe, the tenth part, fills all classical literature, as well as the whole of Holy Scripture. And yet, with all that before our eyes, as plain as plain can be, here we are, at this time of day, blundering about and telling lies, many of us, like Ananias and Sapphira, without any method, or principle, or rule in our givings, any more than if Scripture had never spoken on this matter, or as if a rule of love and common-sense had never been laid down. Till we waken up, and take the Patriarchal, and Mosaic, and Prophetic, and Apostolic, and even Pagan way of taxing our income, and laying aside a definite and a liberal part of it for church and charity, we need never expect to inherit the promises, or to enter into that liberty of heart and hand which awaits us and our children. It is surely time that we had found out some better way than our present haphazard way of dealing with this great and pressing matter. For everything comes on us in this city. All Scotland, all Ireland, and many parts even of rich England; France, Switzerland, Italy; churches, manses, missions—everything comes on Edinburgh, and on a limited field of Edinburgh. When some great financial genius, say, like Dr. Chalmers, arises in the Church to expound and enforce this disastrously neglected law of God, a new day will dawn on our whole religious and charitable exchequer. Then the Christian child will be brought up to tithe his pocket-money of sixpence a week for Jesus his Saviour's sake. And his father his pound a week, or his ten pounds, or his hundred, or his thousand. And, then, all we shall have to do, without straining our hearts or souring our tempers, will be calmly, and at our leisure, to exercise our best discretion as to the proportion and the destination of the stewardship-money we have had intrusted to us.

And, when that Apostolic day dawns, our successors in the churches and charities of the land will look back with amazement at our poverty-stricken ways of collecting church money, leaning on State endowments, and all such like un-Pentecostal expedients. And all because our eyes had, somehow, not been opened to Scriptural wisdom, and to Scriptural love, and to Scriptural liberality, in this whole matter of our Lord's money.

XCII

SIMON MAGUS

BUT who, to begin with, was Simon Magus? And how did it come about that he believed, and was actually baptized by Philip the evangelist; and then was detected, denounced and utterly reprobated by the Apostle Peter? How did all that come about?

Well, you must know that Samaria, where Simon Magus lived and carried on his astounding impositions, was a half-Hebrew, half-heathen country. Samaria had just enough of the Hebrew blood in its veins to make it full of the very worst qualities of that blood, mixed up with some of the very worst qualities of the heathen blood of that day also. And Simon Magus was at once the natural product, and the divine punishment, of that apostate land in which we find him living in such mountebank prosperity. Simon Magus was a very clever man, and he was at the same time a very bad man; till, by his tremendous pretensions, he had the whole of Samaria at his feet. There was something positively sublime about the impudence and charlatanry of Simon Magus, till he was actually

feared and obeyed and worshipped as nothing short
of some divinity who had condescended to come
and take up his abode in Samaria. But the whole
man and the whole situation is best set before us in
the two or three strokes of the sacred writer.
"There was a certain man called Simon, which
beforetime in the same city used sorcery, and
bewitched the people of Samaria, giving out that
himself was some great one. To whom they all
gave heed, from the least to the greatest, saying,
This man is the great power of God. And to him
they had regard, because that of long time he had
bewitched them with sorceries. But when they
believed Philip preaching the things concerning the
kingdom of God, and the name of Jesus Christ,
they were baptized, both men and women. Then
Simon himself believed also; and when he was
baptized, he continued with Philip and wondered,
beholding the miracles and signs which were done."
Philip had extraordinary success in his evangelising
mission to Samaria. It was like New England, or
Cambuslang, or 1859-60, or Moody and Sankey's
first visit to Scotland. For the people with one
accord gave heed unto those things that Philip
spake, hearing and seeing the miracles which he
did. And there was great joy in that city. 'The
very devil himself has been converted and has been
baptized by me,' Philip telegraphed to Jerusalem.
'I actually have the name of Simon Magus on
my communion-roll.' At the hearing of that, the
apostles sent two of their foremost men down to
Samaria to superintend the great movement, and

God sent the Holy Ghost with them, till the whole of Samaria seemed to have turned to God and to the name of Jesus Christ. Only, Simon Magus was all the time such an impostor that in his conversion and baptism he had completely deceived Philip. Nay, I think it but fair to Simon Magus to say that he had completely deceived himself as well as Philip. I think so. I am bound in charity to think so. When Simon Magus came up out of the water, had a voice from heaven spoken at that moment, it would surely have been heard to say, 'This is an arch-deceiver, deceiving, but, at the same time, being deceived.' Some men have far more self-discernment than other men, and self-discernment is the highest and rarest science of all the sciences on the face of the earth. And, usually, there is united with great self-discernment, and as a reward and a premium put by God upon its exercise, the power of deeply discerning other men's spirits also. Now, though Philip was a prince of evangelistic preachers, and a good and an able man, at the same time he was far too easily satisfied with his converts. Philip was far better at preaching than he was at catechising. And thus it was that it fell to Peter and John to purge Philip's communion-roll of Simon Magus immediately on their arrival in Samaria. At the same time, this must be said, that Simon Magus had never come out in his true colours till after Peter's arrival, and till after all the true converts had received the Holy Ghost.

The circumstances were these: It was part of

the Pentecostal equipment of the apostles to possess
for a time some of the miracle-working powers that
their Divine Master had exercised in order to arrest
attention to His advent, and to secure a hearing to
His ministry. And thus it is that we find the
apostles speaking with tongues, healing the sick,
opening the eyes of the blind, casting out devils,
and many suchlike miracles and signs. Now, Simon
Magus, like everybody else in Samaria, was im-
mensely impressed with all that he saw and heard.
No man was more impressed than Simon Magus, or
more convinced of the divine mission of the apostles.
But, with all his wonder and with all his conviction,
he was never truly converted. The love of money,
and the still more intoxicating love of notoriety,
had taken such absolute possession of Simon Magus
that he simply could not live out of the eyes of men.
He must be in men's mouths. He must have a
crowd around him. Themistocles could not sleep
because of the huzzas that filled the streets of Athens
when Miltiades walked abroad ; and the crowds that
followed Peter and John were gall and wormwood
to Simon Magus. For, still greater crowds used to
take him up and carry him on their shoulders in
the days of his great power before Philip came to
Samaria. Now, Peter had never liked the look of
Philip's great convert, and it completely justified
Peter's incurable suspicions when Simon Magus came
one night into Peter's lodgings, and, setting down a
bag of money on the table, said, ' What will you take
for the Holy Ghost ? If you will show me the secret
of your apostleship so that I may work your miracles

like you, I have plenty of money, and I know where there is plenty more.' The sight of the bag, and the blasphemous proposal of the owner of the bag, nearly drove Peter beside himself. And the old fisherman so blazed out at the poor mountebank that the page burns red to this day with Peter's denunciation. " Thy money perish with thee, for I perceive thou art still in the gall of bitterness, and in the bond of iniquity ! "

" Giving out that himself was some great one." That is our first lesson from this Holy Scripture about Simon Magus. Let those take the lesson to heart who specially need it, and who will humble themselves to receive it. It may be in sorcery and witchcraft like that of Simon Magus ; it may be in the honours of the kingdom of Heaven like the sons of Zebedee ; it may be in preaching sermons ; it may be in making speeches or writing books ; it may be in anything you like, down to your child's possessions and performances ; but we all, to begin with, give ourselves out to be some great one. Simon Magus was but an exaggerated specimen of every popularity-hunter among us. There is an element and first principle of Simon Magus, the Samaritan mountebank, in all public men. There is still a certain residuum of Simon left in order to his last sanctification in every minister. But the most Simon Magus-like of all sanctified ministers I know is Thomas Shepard, and that just because he is the most self-discerning, the most honest, and the most outspoken about himself of us all. Popularity was the very breath of life to that charlatan of Samaria. He

o

could not work, he could not live, he could not be
converted and baptized, without popularity. And
there is not one public man in a thousand, politician
or preacher, who will go on living and working and
praying out of sight, and all the time with sweetness, and contentment, and good-will, and a quiet
heart. All Samaria must give heed to Simon Magus
from the least to the greatest. And so still with
his successors. A despairing missionary to the
drunken navvies on a new railway, complained to
me the other day that one of our great preachers,
who was holidaying in the neighbourhood, would
not give an idle Sabbath afternoon hour to the men
loitering about the bothy door. It was the dregs
of Simon Magus in the city orator; he could not
kindle but to a crowd. "Seek obscurity" was
Fénelon's motto. Whether he lived up to his
motto or no, the day will declare; if he did, there
will not be many wearing the same crown with him
on that day. But Richard Baxter will be one of
them. "I am much less regardful of the approba-
tion of men, and set much lighter by contempt or
applause, than I did long ago. All worldly things
appear most vain and unsatisfactory when we have
tried them most. But though I feel that this hath
some hand in the effect, yet the knowledge of man's
nothingness, and of God's transcendent greatness,
with whom it is that I have most to do, and the
sense of the brevity of human things, and the nearness
of eternity, are the principal causes of this effect, and
not self-conceitedness and morosity, as some suppose." These things will help to do it, but above

all these things a completely broken heart will alone cast Simon Magus out of us ministers. A heart broken beyond all mollification or binding up in this world; but not even a broken heart, unless it is daily broken. Nothing will root the mountebank out of us ministers but constant self-detection, constant self-contempt, constant self-denunciation, and constant self-destruction. Oh, my friends, you do not know, and you are not fit to be told, the tremendous price of a minister's salvation. It is this that makes our crucified Master say to us ministers continually, " Few of you there be that find it."

You will not know what a " law-work " is; but Simon Magus was simply lost for want of a law-work. You never nowadays hear the once universal pulpit word. The Romans and the Galatians are full of the law-work, and so have all our greatest preachers been. Those two great evangelical Epistles were not yet written, but there was enough of their contents in the Pentecostal air, if Simon Magus had had any taste for such soul-searching matters. I must not allow myself to say a single word as to Philip's mismanagement of his catechumens' and young communicants' classes. Only, the sorcerer must have sadly bewitched the evangelist before Philip put Simon Magus's name down on his communion-roll. Philip knew his business and his own heart. I dare not doubt that. Only, somehow or other, he let Simon Magus slip through his hands much too easily. Believing, baptism, communion-table and all, Simon Magus had neither part nor lot in this matter of the work of the law. I would

not keep either a young communicant or an old
convert away from the table because he was not
deeply learned in all the Pauline doctrines; but I
could not undertake to recommend his name to the
kirk-session unless he gave me some evidence of
what the masters of our science call the law-work.
He might never have heard the word, and I would
never mention it to him unless, indeed, he was a
man of some mind.   But it is mocking God, and
deluding men, to crowd the table with communicants
like Simon Magus, who do not know the first principles either of sin or of salvation.   The best law-
work comes to us long after conversion and admission
to the table; but neither before his so-called conversion, nor after it, did this arch-impostor know
anything about it—" for thy heart," said Peter,
tearing it open to its very core, " is not right in the
sight of God."

" Fictus," that is to say, a living and breathing
fiction, was the name given to such converts as
Simon Magus in those early days.   Ignorance,
Temporary, Pliable, and Turnaway, were some of
their names in later days.   Now, you are not an
impostor by profession like Simon Magus.   You do
not make your living by deluding other people.
But there may very easily be an element of fiction,
of self-delusion and self-imposition, in your supposed
conversion, as there was in his.   Calvin's moderation,
saneness of judgment, and spiritual insight, carry
me with him here also.   " I am not of their mind,"
he says, " who think that Simon Magus made only
a semblance of religion.   There is a middle ground

between saving faith and sheer dissimulation. Simon Magus saw that the apostles' doctrine was true, and he received the same so far; but the groundwork was all along wanting; that is to say, his denial of himself was all along wanting." Just so. I see and feel Calvin's point. Your religion is not all a sham on your part. You are not a pure and unmixed hypocrite. But neither is your religion of the right kind. It is not saving your soul. It is not making you every day a new and another man. Your heart is not right in the sight of God. It is not, and it never will be, till, as Calvin says, and as Christ says, you deny yourself daily. And that, every day, to your heart's blood, and in the matter of the sin that so easily besets you. With Simon Magus it was the praise of men, and their crowding round him, and their adulation of him. Now, what he should have done, and what Philip should have insisted on him to do, was to discover to himself and to confess to himself his besetting sin, and every day to drive another nail of self-crucifixion into it. Another new nail every day, till it gave up the ghost. Instead of that the poor impostor tried to get Peter to share his apostolic popularity with him for thirty pieces of silver! If you are a platform, or a pulpit, or any other kind of mountebank, seek obscurity, for your soul's salvation lies there. If you are a popular preacher, flee from crowded churches, and hold services in bothies, and in poorhouses, and in barns, and in kitchens. Never search the papers to see what they are saying about you. Starve the self-seeking quack that is still within you. Beat him black and blue, as Paul tells us he did, and as Thomas Shepard tells us he did, every time he shows his self-admiring face.

Simon Magus put the thought of his heart into the form of a money-proposal to Peter. But, bad as the proposal was, it was not so much the proposal that Peter so struck at as the heart of the proposer. "If perhaps the thought of thine heart may be forgiven thee." Now, answer this, as we shall all answer it one day — What about the thoughts of your heart? Are the self-seeking, self-exalting thoughts of your heart dwelt on and indulged, or are they the greatest shame to you, and the greatest torment to you, of your life? Do you hate your own heart as you would hate hell itself, if you were about to be cast down into it? Do you beat your breast and cry out, Oh, wretched man that I am! Has the law entered, and is the law-work deep enough, and spiritual enough, to make all the Simon Magus-like thoughts of your hearts to be an inward pain and shame to you past all knowledge, and past all belief about you, of mortal man? His thoughts, that is, of self-advertisement, self-exaltation, and self-congratulation? Does the praise of men puff you up, and make you very happy? And is their silence, or their absence, something you cannot get over? Is he a good man who follows you about, and believes in you, and applauds you: and is he an unpardonably bad man who prefers Philip, and Peter, and John to Simon Magus? Then, be not deceived, God is not mocked, and neither are the self-discerning men round about you. Both your happiness and your sadness: both your love and your hatred of men; are quite naked and open to those with whom you have to do. "For I perceive that thou art still in the gall of bitterness, and in the bond of iniquity." "We may conjecture," says Calvin, "that Simon Magus repented." Whereas Bengel leaves it to the last day to discover that and to declare that.

XCIII

THE ETHIOPIAN EUNUCH

UR Lord gave the Pharisees of His day
this praise, that they would compass
sea and land to make one proselyte.
Now, this Ethiopian eunuch was one
of their proselytes. Like the Scotch
and English of our own day, the Jews of our Lord's
day compassed sea and land to make money; but,
almost more, to make converts to Moses and Aaron.
Bent as their hearts were on making a fortune, the
Jews of that day were almost more bent on spreading
the faith of Abraham, and the hope of their fathers.
And it would be in his business relations with the
heads of some of the trading and banking houses
that the Jewish merchants had set up in Ethiopia,
that Queen Candace's treasurer came into contact
with the worshippers of Jehovah, till it all ended
in his becoming a proselyte of the gate. Think,
then, of this Ethiopian treasurer and his royal
retinue coming up all the way from the far south
to pay his vow, and to seek the face of the Lord in
His holy temple. Think you see his conversion in
Ethiopia, his sojourning for a season in Jerusalem,
and then his returning home; and these pictures of

him in your mind will greatly help you to understand and appreciate this remarkable man and his
remarkable story.

Now, what the Ethiopian eunuch saw and heard
in Jerusalem, and took home with him from Jerusalem, would almost entirely depend on the introductions he brought with him, and on the houses
to which he took those introductions. If an eastern
prince were to come, say at an Assembly time, to
our own city, his impressions of the city and of the
country would entirely depend on the hands into
which he fell. We are so partitioned off into
churches, and sects, and sub-sects; into professions,
and political parties, and social castes; into likes
and dislikes; into sympathies and into antipathies;
that, if the Ethiopian eunuch had his first introduction into any of those hot-beds of ours, he would
return home a total stranger, and almost an enemy,
to many of the best men and to much of the best
life of our city and our country. Unless indeed, he
had brought from his bitter experience of controversy, and faction, and party spirit in Ethiopia, that
open and liberal mind, and that humble and loving
heart, which no designed introduction will mislead,
and no invidious patronage or privilege will poison.

Had this been an ordinary Ethiopian eunuch he
would have spent his holiday among the theatres,
and circuses, and bazaars, and other Roman amuse-
ments, of Pilate's procuratorship. As it was, he
may, for anything we know, have brought an introduction to the Roman Procurator, and may have
been entertained by Pilate's wife herself in the

Roman Prætorium. On the other hand, it is much more likely that he was directed and recommended to some of the heads of the Temple: to Annas, or to Caiaphas, or to some other ecclesiastical dignitary. You may make use of your own knowledge of the condition of Jerusalem, and of the rank of the eunuch, and of his religious errand, to choose for yourselves just where the Ethiopian eunuch was lodged, and just in what light he saw the life of Jerusalem. Only, I fear, with all his ability, and with all his insight, and with all his seriousness of mind, the eunuch's furlough came to an end before he had well begun to see daylight on the Pharisees and the Sadducees, the Essenes and the Herodians, the Zelots and the Publicans, the devotees of Moses, and the disciples of Jesus Christ.

Was the Book of the prophet Isaiah the parting gift of his Jerusalem host to this eastern prince on the day of his departure home? And did the donor of the sacred book, with an earnest look and with delicate kindness, point out to his guest as he mounted his chariot steps, the fifty-third and fifty-sixth chapters of the evangelical and ecumenical prophet? Or was the sacred book this good eunuch's own selection? After he had purchased some of the rarest specimens of recent Roman art for his royal mistress, did he seek out the sacred scriptorium and price for himself the richest-set roll of the prophet Esaias that the scribes possessed? In whatever way he had come by the fascinating book, he was away out of the city, and well on to the border of the land, before he was able to take

his eyes off his purchase. The Ethiopian eunuch
will be summoned forward with his Isaiah in his
hand at the last day to witness against us all for
the books we buy and read, and for the way we
murder time, both at home and on our holidays,
as well as on our long journeys. Did you ever see
any one reading his Bible in a railway carriage,
or on the deck of a steamboat? Did you ever
see Isaiah, or Paul, in text or in commentary,
exposed for sale on a railway bookstall? Oh, no!
the very thought is profanity. We load our book-
stalls, and our newsboys' baskets, and our travelling-
bags, with all the papers of the morning and the evening; and with piles of novels of all colours; and with
our well-known Protestant reticence and reverence
for divine things, we reserve our Bibles for home,
and give up our Sabbath-days to Paul and Isaiah.
One in a thousand will break through and will re-read
on a railway journey his Homer or his Virgil; his
Milton or his Shakespeare; his Bacon or his Hooker;
his À Kempis or his Bunyan; while one in a hundred thousand will venture to take out his Psalms
or his New Testament. " The great number of books
and papers of amusement, which of one kind or
another, daily come in one's way, have in part
occasioned, and most perfectly fall in with, and
humour, this idle way of reading and considering
things. By this means time, even in solitude,
is happily got rid of, without the pain of attention.
Neither is any part of it more put to the account
of idleness—one can scarce forbear saying is spent
with less thought, than great part of that which is

spent in reading." If that accusation was laid
against the readers of 1792, how much more have
we laid ourselves open to it in 1899?

But, all this time Philip is wandering up and
down the wilderness, thinking that he must have
mistaken his own imagination for the voice of the
Lord. Caravans of pilgrims come and go: merchants
of Egypt and of Arabia and cohorts of Roman
soldiers. but all that only makes the evangelist
the more lonely and the more idle. But, at last,
a chariot of distinction comes in sight, and as it
comes within earshot Philip hears with the utmost
astonishment the swarthy master of the chariot
reading aloud. Philip was not astonished at the
distinguished man reading aloud, but his astonishment and admiration were unbounded when he
began to make out at a distance what the dark-
skinned stranger was reading. "He was led as a
sheep to the slaughter; and like a lamb dumb before
his shearer, so opened he not his mouth." "Understandest thou what thou readest?" said Philip, as
the chariot came to a standstill. All this took
place in the simple, unsophisticated, hospitable
East; and it must not be measured by our hard
and unbending habits of intercourse in the West;
and, especially, in dour-faced Scotland. It would
be taken as the height of intrusion, and, indeed,
impudence, among us if one man said to another
sitting over his book on a journey, "Are you understanding what you are reading?" But if we sat
beside a foreigner who was struggling with one of
our complicated guide-books, and was just about to

"Understandest thou what thou readest?"

start off in a wrong direction, it would be no intrusion if we leaned over and said to him, 'I fear,
sir, that our barbarous language is not easily
mastered by foreign scholars; but English is my
native tongue, and I belong to this country. Can
I be of any use to you?' "How can I," said the
eunuch, "except some man should guide me?"
And he desired Philip that he would come up and
sit with him. Had the eunuch come to Jerusalem
last year at this passover time, as he had been
urged to come, and as he had at one time intended
to come, he might have had Philip's Master sitting
beside him to-day and reading Isaiah with him.
But the eunuch had missed that opportunity by
putting off paying his vow for another year. He was
a year too late for ever seeing Jesus Christ in the
flesh, and hearing Him open up Isaiah concerning
Himself. But, better late than never. Better
meet the meanest of His servants, than miss the
Master altogether.

Was it the eunuch's own serious instincts, I
wonder, that led him to the fifty-third of Isaiah?
Or had he heard that profound and perplexing
chapter disputed over by Stephen and Saul in one
of the synagogues of Jerusalem? I cannot tell.
Only, it strikes me, and it struck Philip, as a remarkable fact that out of the whole Old Testament
this utter stranger to the Old Testament was pon-
dering over its most central chapter, and its most
profound prophecy, as he rode home in his chariot.
When Augustine was a catechumen in Milan, and
was just at the eunuch's stage in the truth, Ambrose

directed his pupil to the study of Isaiah. "But I, not understanding my first lesson in that prophet, laid it by to be resumed when I was better practised." Bunyan also tells us that when he was beginning to read his Bible he much preferred the adventures of Joshua and Samson and Gideon to Isaiah or Paul. But, explain it as we may, this Ethiopian neophyte was already far ahead of Bunyan, and even of Augustine. For he held in his hands the most Pauline page in all the Old Testament, and he would not lay it down till he got to the bottom of it. "I pray thee, of whom speaketh the prophet this? of himself, or of some other man?" What struck the imagination and the conscience of the eunuch was this: the absolutely unearthly picture that the prophet draws of his own character and conduct: if indeed it is of his own character and conduct the prophet speaks. "He was led as a sheep to the slaughter," the eunuch read again, "and like a lamb dumb before his shearer, so opened he not his mouth." The eunuch knew not a few good, and humble, and patient, and silently-suffering, men in Ethiopia, but he knew no one of whom the half of these things could be said. And, if this was the prophet himself, no wonder then at the reverence in which both the name of the prophet, and the name of his book, were held in Jerusalem. 'Oh, no!' said Philip. 'Oh, no, no! the prophet did not speak of himself, nor of any other mortal man. Oh, no, no! far from that! The prophet was a man of like passions with other men. He was a man of unclean lips,

like all other men. Oh, no! the prophet did not
speak of himself, but of another manner of man
altogether. Thou art a stranger in Jerusalem, but
thou must have heard something of the things that
have come to pass there in these last days. Thou
must surely have heard the name of Jesus of
Nazareth?' 'I did hear that name,' answered the
eunuch. 'I often heard it. Sometimes I heard
that name blessed, and sometimes I heard it cursed.
And I was warned that all the time I was in
Jerusalem I must not once speak that name, nor
listen to any one speaking it to me. But we are
far from Jerusalem here; and of whom speaketh
the prophet this?' "Should we make it our first
aim in the pulpit to do full justice to the subject
we have in hand; or should our immediate and sole
endeavour be to do good to our hearers?" said one
of my most thoughtful friends to me the other
day. What do you do yourself? was my reply to
him. But we had to part before we had time to
argue it out. Philip, at any rate, set himself in
the first place, and with all his might, to do full
justice to his great subject. And it was in the
progress of that full justice that the eunuch got
all the good that the best hearer even in our day
could get from the best preacher. Sometimes the
one way is best, in some hands, and sometimes
the other, according to the preacher, according to
the hearer, and according to the subject. For the
most part surely, first the subject thoroughly studied
down, and handled with our utmost ability and
finish, and then application made with our utmost

skill and urgency and love. "Mix your exhortation with doctrine," said Goodwin to the divinity
students of Oxford. Better still, in our day at any
rate, begin your exhortation well with doctrine, and
then end your doctrine with its proper exhortation
springing out of it. Only, the eunuch did not wait
for Philip's exhortation. He did not give Philip
time to wind up and round off his doctrine. Philip's
sermon on the fifty-third of Isaiah is not finished
to this day. "See, here is water!" broke in the
eunuch. "I see it!" broke in a young Forfar-
shire farmer in the middle of my prayer with him
in the minister's study late that night after a fine
revival meeting conducted by Mr. Low of Fountain-
bridge, and Dr. Macphail of Liverpool. And my
prayer lies there to this day, like Philip's sermon,
never finished, and that is five-and-twenty years
ago. "I see it!" and we both sprang to our feet;
and, instead of the rest of my prayer to God I
said to the farmer, "Never lose sight of it, then.
Never lose sight of it all your days!" He did lose
sight of it, and went back, to the breaking of his
minister's heart. But the backslider returned, and,
as I was told, died in raptures, exclaiming, "I see
it! I see it!" "See, here is water!" exclaimed
the eunuch, cutting short Philip's sermon. "I see
it!" exclaimed the farmer, cutting short my prayer.

"And when they were come up out of the water,
the Spirit of the Lord caught away Philip, that the
eunuch saw him no more; and he went on his way
rejoicing." Rejoicing that those Jewish merchants
had ever opened their warehouse in Ethiopia

Regretting that he had not come up sooner to Jerusalem, when he might have seen his Saviour's face, and heard His voice. But, all the more rejoicing that he had not put off coming to the passover altogether. Rejoicing also that he had not talked about the sights of Jerusalem all the way to Gaza, but had read all the way in the prophet Isaiah. And rejoicing, above all, that he had said it the moment it came into his heart to say it, "See, here is water!" And, still, as the chariot travelled its long stages toward far Ethiopia, the eunuch thought with a humble and a holy joy of all the way his God had led him, and of the singular grace that had at last apprehended him. And who can tell but that Queen Candace, and a great multitude of her black, but comely people, will yet be seen by us stretching out their hands and casting their crowns at His feet of whom Isaiah spake, and of whom Philip preached!

> Let it no longer be a forlorn hope
>   To wash an Ethiope;
> He's washed : his gloomy skin a peaceful shade
>   For his white soul is made.
> And now, I doubt not, the Eternal Dove,
>   A black-faced house will love.

P

XCIV

GAMALIEL

READ for the first time, and looked at on the surface, Gamaliel's speech in the council of Jerusalem was both an able and a successful performance. The argument of the speech carried the consent of the whole council—not an easy thing to do—for Peter had just cut the whole council to the heart. But Gamaliel calmed the whole council; he reassured the most hesitating; and he all but satisfied the most bloodthirsty; till the whole Sanhedrim broke up that day with loud and universal congratulations pronounced upon the ability and the sagacity of Gamaliel's speech. But, in order to see what was the real and ultimate value of Gamaliel's speech; and, still more, in order to a true and ultimate estimate of Gamaliel himself, let us look with some closeness at the whole situation with which Gamaliel was called upon to deal that day.

Well, then, this was the situation. Gamaliel had brought forward Theudas, who had boasted that he was somebody; and Judas of Galilee, who had drawn away much people after him; and

Gamaliel had made some good points in his speech
by his references to those two dispersed men. But
Jesus Christ was not a Theudas, nor a Judas of
Galilee, nor a dispersed man. Jesus Christ was
Jesus Christ. He was Himself, and not another.
Jesus Christ had been promised in every page of the
law and the prophets and the psalms, all of which
were the daily text-books in Gamaliel's school. And
Jesus Christ had come, and had fulfilled, and that
a thousand times told, every jot and tittle of all that
had been prophesied and promised concerning Him.
And Gamaliel had been set in his high seat by the
God of Israel in order that he might watch for the
coming Messiah, and might announce His advent
to the people of Israel. But, for some reason or
other, instead of recognising and announcing the
true Christ of God when He came, as, for instance,
John the Baptist did; instead of casting in his lot
with Jesus of Nazareth; instead of dissolving his
school and sending Saul of Tarsus and all his other
scholars to follow the Lamb of God, Gamaliel, for
some reason or other, still kept his seat in the
Sanhedrim all through the arrest, the trial, the
crucifixion, the resurrection, and the ascension of
Jesus Christ, and when Christ's disciples were on
their trial for their lives this short speech contains
all that Gamaliel has to say for them and for
himself. We must, at all times, and to all men, do
as we would be done by: and therefore it is that
we seek again and again for some explanation, some
excuse, some apology, for Gamaliel's remaining a
member of the council that had tried and crucified

Jesus Christ. But, with all our search, we can find nothing out of which to make a cloak for Gamaliel's case. Had Gamaliel been an ignorant and an unlearned man there might have been some excuse for him. But Gamaliel had not that cloak at any rate for his sin. So far as I can see it, the simple truth in Gamaliel's deplorable case was this. With all his learning, and with all his ability, and with all his address, Gamaliel had approached this whole case concerning Jesus Christ from the wrong side; he had taken hold of this whole business by the wrong handle. And we all make Gamaliel's tremendous and irreparable mistake when we approach Jesus Christ and His cause and His kingdom on the side of policy, and when we handle Him as a matter open to argument and debate. He is not a matter of argument and debate; He is an ambassador of reconciliation. We are simply not permitted to sit in judgment on Almighty God, and on His message of mercy to us. He who sends that message to us is our Maker and our Judge. And Gamaliel, with all his insight, and with all his lawyer-like ability, has turned all things completely upside down when he sits in judgment, and gives this carefully-balanced caution, concerning the Son of God.

Speaking philosophically and politically and ecclesiastically, Gamaliel was a liberal, and he has this to be said for him, that he was a liberal long before the time. He was all for toleration, and for a free church in a free state, in an intolerant and persecuting day. He was far in advance of his colleagues in observation, and in reading, and in breadth and openness of mind. He was tinctured with the Greek learning that so many of his class were now beginning innovatingly to taste. And we cannot but wonder whether, among all his stores of ancient instances, that of the Greek Socrates had come that day into his mind. "We ought to obey God rather than men," Peter had just said. "Whether it be right in the sight of God to hearken unto you rather than unto Him, judge ye," he had also said. "Athenians," said Socrates, "I hold you in the highest reverence and love; but I will obey God rather than you. I cannot hold my peace, because that would be to disobey God." And Socrates continued so to obey God till his self-examining voice was put to silence in the hemlock-cup. And much more must Peter summon all Jerusalem to repentance in spite of the prison and the scourge and the cross. The Athenians, in their philosophical and political liberality, would have let Socrates alone, if he would have let them alone; but not for his life could he do that. And Peter was under a far surer and a far stronger constraint than Socrates. The one was the apostle of truth as it is in the reason, and in the conscience, and in the self-examined heart; while the other was the apostle of the truth as it is in all that, and in Jesus over and above all that. The French, with their keen, quick, caustic wit, have coined a nickname for those politicians who neglect principles and study the skies only to see how the wind is to blow. They call all such public men by the biting name of "opportunists." Now, Gamaliel

was the opportunist of the council of Jerusalem in
that day.   He was a politician, but he was not a
true churchman or statesman.   He was held in
repute by the people; but the people were blind,
and they loved to be led by blind leaders.   And
Gamaliel was one of them.   For, at this supreme
crisis of his nation's history, when there was not
another moment to lose, this smooth-tongued
opportunist came forward full of wise saws and
modern instances.   But the flood was out, and the
time was past, if ever there was a time for such fatal
counsellors as Gamaliel.   His own opportunity has
of late been passing with lightning-speed: and, now,
when God, in His long-suffering, has given Gamaliel
his last opportunity, he deals with God and with his
own soul as we here see.

Erasmus and the Reformation always rise before
me when I read of Gamaliel and study his character.
Erasmus, the fastidious, cautious, cool, almost cold
scholar.   Always stepping lightly over thin ice,
always calculating consequences, and always missing
the mark.   Convinced of the truth, but a timid
friend to the truth.   Clear-eyed enough to see the
truth, but built without a brow for it.   Lavater
thus analyses Holbein's portrait of Erasmus, and as
we read the remarkable analysis we see in it a replica
of Gamaliel's portrait.—" The face is expressive of
the man.   There is a pose of feature indicative of
timidity, hesitancy, circumspection.   There is in the
eye the calm serenity of the acute observer who sees
and takes in all things.   The half-closed eye, of such
a depth and shape, is surely such as always belongs

to the subtle and clever schemer. That nose, according to all my observation, is assuredly that of a man of keen intellect and delicate sensibility. The furrows on the brow are usually no favourable token : they are almost invariably the sign of some weakness, some carelessness, some supineness, some laxness of character. We learn, however, from this portrait that they are to be found in some great men." Altogether a man of maxims and not of morals; a man, as he said of himself, who had no inclination to die for the truth : a man, as Luther said of him, in whose estimation human things stood higher than divine things : a man, two men, Gamaliel and Erasmus, a large class of men. " Speak not of them," said the master, " but look at them and pass them by."

Young men! with your life still before you, Gamaliel, the fluent and applauded opportunist, is here written with a special eye to your learning. Make your choice. It is an awful thing to say, but it is the simple truth ; God and His Son, His church and His gospel, His cause and His kingdom, all stand before your door at this moment, waiting for your choice and your decision. Gamaliel decided, and his day is past, and he is in his own place. And now is your day of decision. Everlasting and irremediable issues for you and for others depend on this day's decision. Make up your minds. Take the step. Take sides with Peter and John. Take sides with Jesus Christ. And, as time goes on, having taken that side, that step will solve for you a thousand perplexities, and will deliver you from a thousand snares. You will be the children of the light and of the day: and you will walk in the light when other men all around you are stumbling in darkness, and know not whither they are going. Suppose that you had been Gamaliel, and act now as you so clearly see how he should have acted then.

This is our sacrament evening, and we have come to Gamaliel, and to his choice, and to his speech, not inopportunely, as I think, for our ensample on such an evening. For, what is a sacrament, and a sacrament day, and a sacrament evening? Well, Gamaliel may very well have seen the sacramental oath taken by the young soldiers under the walls of Jerusalem. At any rate, if he had ever been at Rome on a deputation, he would to a certainty have seen and heard the Sacramentum sworn to on the field of Mars. For the Sacramentum was the well-known military oath that the young soldier took when he entered on his place in the world-conquering legions of Rome. It was his sacramental oath when he lifted up his hand to heaven and swore that he would follow the eagles of Cæsar wherever they flew; to the swamps of Germany, to the snows of Caledonia, to the sands of Arabia, to the Jordan, to the Nile, to the Ganges, to the Thames, to the Clyde, to the Tay. And we, this day, old soldiers of the cross, and new recruits alike, have called upon God and man to see us that we will not flinch from the cross, but will follow it to heat and cold, to honour and shame, to gain and loss, to life and death. We have eagles to fight under, of which the

angels desire to be the camp-followers. Only, let
us all well understand, and without any possibility
of mistake, just where our field of battle lies; just
who and what is our enemy, just who is our Captain,
just what is His whole armour, and just what hope
He holds out to us of victory.

Well, then, lay this to heart, that your battlefield
is not over the seas: it is at home. It is in the
family, it is in the office, it is in the shop, it is in
the workshop, it is at the breakfast and dinner-
table, it is in the class-room, it is in the council-
chamber. Your battlefield is just where you are.
Your battle follows you about the world, and it is
set just where you are set. And that is because
your enemy, and the enemy of your Captain, is
yourself. It is no paradox to say that; it is no
hyperbole, no extravagance, no exaggeration. "The
just understand it of their passions," says Pascal.
That is to say, they understand that their only
enemy is their own sensuality, their own bad
temper, their own hot and hasty and unrecalled
words, their own resentment of injuries, their own
retaliation, their own revenge, their own implacable
ill-will, their own envy of their dearest friend when
he excels them in anything—and so on. What a
sacramental oath that is, to swear to take no rest,
and to give God no rest, till He has rooted all these,
and all other enemies of His and ours, out of our
heart! But, then, let us think of our Captain, and of
our armour, and of our rations, as in this house this
day, and of our battle-cry, and of our sure and
certain victory. And, then, eye hath not seen, nor

ear heard, the things that God hath prepared for
him that overcometh. "To him that overcometh
will I grant to sit with Me in My throne, even as
I also overcame, and am set down with My Father
in His throne."

XCV

BARNABAS

BARNABAS, I am afraid, is little more than a bare name to the most of us. Paul so eclipses every one of his contemporaries, that it is with the utmost difficulty we can get a glimpse of any one but Paul. How much do you know about Barnabas? Who was Barnabas? Why was Joses called Barnabas? You would have some difficulty, I am afraid, in giving answers to all these questions. And I do not blame you for your ignorance of Barnabas. For, Paul is so great, that the very greatest and the very best men look but small when placed alongside of him. At the same time, there were great men before Agamemnon, and Barnabas was one of them.

"Barnabas, a Levite, of the country of Cyprus, having land, sold it, and brought the money, and laid it at the apostles' feet." Cyprus is a large and fertile island situated off the coast of Syria. In ancient times Cyprus was famous for its wines, its wheats, its oils, its figs, and its honey. To possess land in Cyprus was to be a rich and an influential man. Many men who possessed houses and lands

sold them under the Pentecostal fervour, and laid
their prices at the apostles' feet. But Barnabas
stood at the head of them all; such was his great
wealth, such was his great generosity, such was his
high character, and such were his splendid services
in this and in many other ways to the apostolic
church.

As we read on in the Acts of the Apostles we
come to the sad story of Ananias and Sapphira;
then to the creation of the office of the deaconship;
then to the great services and the triumphant
translation of Stephen; and, then, the east begins
to break in the conversion of Saul of Tarsus. And
it is in the first rays of that fast-rising sun that we
see for once, if not again, the full stature and the
true nobility of Barnabas. It was but yesterday
that Saul was seen setting out for Damascus,
breathing out threatenings and slaughter against
the disciples of the Lord. And, to-day, he has
fled back to Jerusalem, the most hated, the most
feared, and the most friendless man in all that city.
And, with the blood of so many martyrs still on
his hands, it was no wonder that the disciples in
Jerusalem were all afraid of Saul, and would not
believe that he really intended to be a disciple.
Saul of Tarsus a disciple of Jesus Christ! Saul
of Tarsus converted, and baptized, and preaching
Jesus Christ! No! Depend upon it, this is but
another deep-set snare for our feet! This is but
another trap baited for us by our bitter enemies!
So all the disciples said concerning Saul, and they
all bore themselves to Saul accordingly.

Barnabas alone of all the disciples and apostles
in Jerusalem opened his door to Saul. Barnabas
alone held out his hand to Saul. Barnabas alone
believed Saul's wonderful story of his conversion
and baptism. Barnabas alone rejoiced in God's
saving mercy to Saul's soul. "They were all afraid
of Saul, and believed not that he was a disciple.
But Barnabas took Saul, and brought him to the
apostles, and declared unto them how he had seen
the Lord in the way to Damascus, and that the
Lord had spoken to him, and how he had preached
boldly at Damascus in the name of Jesus Christ."
If Barnabas had never done anything else but what
he did in those days for Saul of Tarsus, he would
deserve, and he would receive, our love and our
honour for ever. Barnabas so firmly believed what
Saul told him, and so nobly acted on it. He so
stood up for Saul when all men were looking
askance at him. He so trusted and befriended
Saul when every one else suspected him, and cast
his past life in his face. Barnabas staked all his
good name in Jerusalem, and all his influence with
the apostles, on the genuineness of Saul's conversion, and on the sincerity and integrity of his
discipleship. Barnabas stood by Saul till he had
so turned the tide in Saul's favour, that, timid as
Peter was, he actually took Saul to lodge with him
in his own house in Jerusalem. And Barnabas
gave Saul up to Peter, only too glad to see Saul
made so much of by such a pillar of the Apostolic
Church as Peter was. With Saul staying fifteen
days under Peter's roof, and with James treating

Saul with his cautious confidence, Barnabas's battle for Saul was now completely won. Very soon, now, it will be the greatest honour to any house on the face of the earth to entertain the apostle Paul. But no proud householder of them all can ever steal this honour from Barnabas, that he was the first man of influence and responsibility who opened his heart and his house to Saul of Tarsus, when all Jerusalem was still casting stones at him. Barnabas was not predestinated to shine in the service of Christ and His Church like Paul; but Paul himself never did a more shining deed than Barnabas did when he took Saul to his heart at a time when every other heart in Jerusalem was hardened against him. Everlastingly well done, thou true son of consolation!

The scene now shifts to Antioch, which is soon to eclipse Jerusalem herself, and to become the true mother-church of evangelical Christianity. The apostolic preaching had an instantaneous and an immense success at Antioch, and it was its very success that raised there also, and with such acuteness, all those doctrinal and disciplinary disputes that fill with such distress the book of the Acts, and the earlier Epistles of Paul. Jerusalem still remained the Metropolitan Church, and the difficulties that had arisen in Antioch were accordingly sent up to Jerusalem for advice and adjudication. And, that the heads of the Church at Jerusalem chose Barnabas out of the whole college of the apostles to go down and examine into the affairs of Antioch, is just another illustration of the high

standing that Barnabas had, both as a man of
marked ability, and of high Christian character.
" Who, when he came, and had seen the grace of
God was glad, and exhorted them all, that with purpose of heart they would cleave unto the Lord.   For
he was a good man, and full of the Holy Ghost and
faith; and much people was added unto the Lord."
How full of the Holy Ghost Barnabas was we are
made immediately to see.   For Barnabas had not
been long in Antioch till he became convinced that
Antioch was very soon to hold the key of the
whole Christian position.   Already, indeed, so many
questions of doctrine and administration were come
to such a crisis in the Church of Antioch, that
Barnabas felt himself quite unable to cope with
them.   And, worse than that, he could not think
of any one in Jerusalem who was any better able
to cope with those difficult questions than he was
himself.   In all Barnabas's knowledge of men, and
it was not narrow, he knew only one man who was
equal to the great emergency at Antioch, and that
man was no other than Saul of Tarsus.   But, then,
Saul was comparatively young as yet; he was not
much known, and he was not much trusted.   And
shall Barnabas take on himself the immense responsibility, and, indeed, immense risk, of sending
for Saul of Tarsus, and bringing him to Antioch?
And shall Barnabas take this great step without
first submitting Saul's name to the authorities at
Jerusalem?   There were great risks in both of
these alternatives, and Barnabas had to act on his
own judgment and conscience and heart.   There

are supreme moments in the field when an officer of original genius, and of the requisite strength of character, will determine to stake all, and to do some bold deed, on his own single responsibility. He will take an immense and an irretrievable step without orders, and, sometimes, against orders. He will thus win the battle, and then he will not mind much either the praise or the blame that comes to him for his successful act of disobedience. Antioch must have Saul of Tarsus; and Barnabas, taking counsel with no one but himself, set out to Tarsus to seek for Saul. "Leaving France, I retired into Germany expressly for the purpose of being able to enjoy in some obscure corner the repose I had always desired, and which had so long been denied me. And I had resolved to continue in the same obscurity, till at length William Farel detained me at Geneva, and that not so much by counsel and exhortation, as by a dread imprecation, which I felt to be as if God from heaven laid His mighty hand upon me to arrest me. For after having learned that my heart was set upon devoting myself to my private studies, for which I wished to keep myself free from all other engagements, and finding that he could gain nothing by entreating me, he proceeded to utter an imprecation that God would curse my retirement, and would blast my selfish studies, if I should refuse to come to Geneva when the need was so great." John Calvin was Saul of Tarsus over again. William Farel was Barnabas over again. And the reformed city of Geneva was the evangelised city of Antioch over again. "Then

departed Barnabas to Tarsus to seek for Saul. And
when he had found him, he brought him to Antioch."
To have the heart to discover a more talented man
than yourself, and then to have the heart to go to
Tarsus for him, and to make way for him in Antioch,
is far better than to have all Saul's talents, and all
the praise and all the rewards of those talents to
yourself. Speaking for myself I would far rather
have a little of Barnabas's grace than have all Saul's
genius. Give me Barnabas's self-forgetful heart,
and let who will undertake Saul's so extraordinary,
but so perilous, endowments. Luther says that we
cannot help being jealous of the men who are in our
own circle and are more talented than ourselves.
Perhaps not. But if Barnabas had to get over
any jealousy in connection with Saul's coming to
Antioch, that jealousy, at any rate, did not hinder
him from setting out to Tarsus to seek for Saul.
He must increase, but I must decrease, said Barnabas
to himself and to his subordinates as he set his face
steadfastly to go down to Tarsus. Barnabas had
taken his own measure accurately, and he had taken
Saul's measure accurately also, and he took action
accordingly. Now, noble conduct like that of
Barnabas is always its own best reward. Christ-
like conduct like that instantly reacts on character,
and character like Barnabas's character manifests
itself in more and more of such Christ-like conduct.
Barnabas had done Saul a good turn before now,
and that only made him the more ready to do him
this new good turn when the opportunity was
afforded him. " Barnabas was a good man, and

full of the Holy Ghost and faith." And three
times he publicly proved that; first, when he sold
his estate in Cyprus and brought the money, and
laid it at the apostles' feet. And he proved that
again when he took Saul in his friendlessness and
brought him to the apostles in Jerusalem, and
compelled them to believe in Saul, and to trust him,
and to employ him. And still more conclusively
did Barnabas prove his fulness of the Holy Ghost,
when he set out to Tarsus to seek for Saul in order
that Saul might come to Antioch, and there super-
sede and extinguish Barnabas himself.

But, as if to chasten our too great pride in Barnabas, even Barnabas, this so pentecostal and so
apostolic man; even Barnabas, so full hitherto of
the Holy Ghost and of faith—even he must fall at
last, and that too all but fatally. For God speaketh
once, yea twice, yet man perceiveth it not, that He
may withdraw man from his purpose, and hide
pride from man. We would have been too much
lifted up to-night about Barnabas if we had not
had his whole history written to us down to the
end. For, what two chosen and fast friends in all
the New Testament circle of friends, would you have
wagered would be the last to fall out fiercely, and
to turn their backs on one another for ever? Not
Paul and Barnabas, at any rate, you would confi-
dently and proudly have said. Whoever will quarrel,
and fall out, and forget what they owe to one an
other, that can never, by any possibility, happen to
Paul and his old patron Barnabas—so you would
have said. But you would have lost your wager,

and your confidence in the best of men to boot.
"Let us go," said Paul to Barnabas, "and visit our
brethren in every city where we have preached the
word of the Lord and see how they do." And Barnabas determined to take with him John, whose
surname was Mark. And Paul thought not good
to take Mark with them. And the contention was
so sharp between them that they departed asunder
the one from the other. And Barnabas took Mark,
and Paul chose Silas. Has Paul forgotten all that
he once owed to Barnabas? And why does Barnabas's so sweet and so holy humility so fail him
when he is so far on in the voyage of life? "Mariners near the shore," says Shepard, "should be on
the outlook for rocks." And Barnabas was so near
the shore by this time that it distresses us sorely to
see his ship strike the rocks and stagger in the sea
in this fashion. Barnabas's ship strikes the rocks
till one of the noblest characters in the New Testament is shattered and all but sunk under our very
eyes. Who was right and who was wrong in this
sharp contention I have no heart to ask. Both
were wrong. Paul, and Barnabas, and Mark too—
all three were wrong. And multitudes in the
Apostolic churches who heard of the scandal, and
took contending sides in it, were wrong also. And
this sad story is told us to this day, not that we
may take sides in it, but that the like of it may
never again happen amongst ourselves.

> The grey-haired saint may fail at last,
> The surest guide a wanderer prove;
>   Death only binds us fast
>   To the bright shore of love.

The last time we see Barnabas, sad to say, Paul and he are contending again. But I will not draw you into that contention. We have had instruction, and example, and warning, and rebuke, enough out of Barnabas already. Instruction and example in Barnabas's splendid liberality with his Cyprus possessions. Instruction and example in his openness and hospitality of mind and heart toward a suspected and a friendless man. And still more instruction and example in his noble absence of all envy and all jealousy of a man far more gifted, far more successful, and soon to be far more famous than himself. And, then, this warning and this rebuke also, that at the end of such a life, even Paul and Barnabas should contend so sharply with one another that they scandalised the whole Church of Christ, and departed asunder never to meet again, unless it was to dispute again in this world.

> Let not the people be too swift to judge,
> As one who reckons on the blades in field
> Or ere the crop be ripe. For I have seen
> The thorn frown rudely all the winter long
> And after bear the rose upon its top ;
> And barque, that all the way across the sea,
> Ran straight and speedy, perish at the last,
> Even in the haven's mouth.

The evening praises the day, and the chief grace of the theatre is the last scene. Be thou faithful unto death, and I will give thee a crown of life.

XCVI

JAMES THE LORD'S BROTHER

 OFTEN imagine myself to be James. I far oftener imagine myself to be in James's place and experience, than in the place and experience of any other man in the whole Bible, or in the whole world. The first thirty years of James's life fascinate me and enthral me far more than all the rest of human life and human history taken together. And I feel sure that I am not alone in that fascination of mine. Who, indeed, would not be absolutely captivated, fascinated, and enthralled, both in imagination and in heart, at the thought of holding James's relationship to Jesus Christ! For thirty years eating every meal at the same table with Him; working six days of the week in the same workshop with Him; going up on the seventh day to the same synagogue with Him; and once every year going up to Jerusalem to the same passover with Him. For James was, actually, the Lord's brother. Not in a figure of speech. Not mystically and spiritually. But literally and actually—he was James the Lord's brother. Jesus was Mary's first-born son, and James was her second son. And the child James would be

the daily delight of his elder Brother; he would be
His continual charge and joy; just as you see two
such brothers in your own family life at home.
When Mary's first-born Son was twelve years old it
was the law of Moses that He should be taken
up to Jerusalem to His first passover. James was
not old enough yet for his first passover, but you
may be sure he missed nothing with his father and
mother and Brother to tell him all about Jerusalem
and the passover when they came home ; James both
hearing his elder Brother and asking Him questions.
For the next eighteen years Joseph's door is her-
metically shut to our holy curiosity. All we know
is, that one, at any rate, of Joseph's household was
filled with wisdom, and the grace of God was upon
Him. Not another syllable more is told us about
Joseph or Mary, or any of their household, till the
preaching of the Baptist broke in on that house, as
on all the houses of the land, like the coming of the
kingdom of heaven. John and his baptism was the
talk of week-day and Sabbath-day in Nazareth,
as in all the land, till at last a company of young
carpenters and fishermen went south to Bethabara
beyond Jordan where John was baptizing. And
Jesus of Nazareth, known as yet by that name only,
was one of them. You have by heart all that immediately took place at the Jordan. " Behold the
Lamb of God, which taketh away the sin of the
world. We have found the Messiah. We have
found Him, of whom Moses in the law, and the
prophets, did write, Jesus of Nazareth, the son of
Joseph. Rabbi, Thou art the Son of God, Thou

art the King of Israel. And Jesus returned in the
power of the Spirit into Galilee. And He came to
Nazareth where He was brought up; and, as His
custom was, He went into the synagogue on the
Sabbath-day and stood up for to read. And there
was delivered to Him the book of the prophet
Esaias. And when He had opened the book He
found the place where it was written, The Spirit of
the Lord is upon Me, because He hath anointed Me
to preach the gospel to the poor; He hath sent Me
to heal the broken-hearted, to preach deliverance to
the captive, and recovering of sight to the blind, to
set at liberty them that are bound, to preach the
acceptable year of the Lord. And all bear Him
witness, and wondered at the gracious words which
proceeded out of His mouth." But, all the time,
James His brother did not believe on Him. No,
nor did James believe down to the very end. I wish
I had the learning and the genius to let you see and
hear all that must have gone on in Joseph's house for
the next three years. The family perplexities about
Jesus; the family reasonings about Him; the family
divisions and disputes about Him; their intoxicating
hopes at one time over Him, and their fears and
sinkings of heart because of Him at another time.
Think out for yourselves those three years, the like
of which never came to any other family on the face
of the earth. And, then, think of the last week of
all; the arrest, the trial, the crucifixion, the resurrection of Mary's first-born Son—whose imagination
is sufficient to picture to itself Joseph and Mary and
James and the other brothers and sisters of Jesus all

that week! Where did they make ready to eat the
passover? What were they doing at the hour when
He was in Gethsemane? Were they standing with
the crowd in the street when He was led about all
night in His bonds? And where were they while
He was being crucified? For, by that time, no one
believed on Him but the thief on the cross alone. All
the faith in Christ that survived the cross was bound
up in that bundle of smoking flax, the penitent and
praying thief. The next time we come on James is
in these golden words of Paul written concerning
him long afterwards, "and that Jesus Christ was
buried, and that He rose the third day according to
the scriptures. After that, He was seen of James;
then of all the apostles." He was seen of James
somewhere, and to somewhat of the same result, that
He was seen of Saul at the gate of Damascus.

Three years pass on, during the progress of which
James has risen to be one of the pillars of the Church
of Jerusalem. James's high character, and his close
relationship to Jesus Christ, taken together with his
conservative tone of mind, all combined to give him
his unique position of influence and authority in
the Church of Jerusalem. We have a life-like
portrait of James as he appeared to the men of
his day which it will interest and impress you to
look at for a moment. "Now, James was holy
from his mother's womb. He drank no wine or
strong drink. He ate no animal food. No razor ever
went on his head. He anointed not himself with
oil, and used not the indulgence of the bath. He
wore no wool, but linen only, and he was such a

man of prayer that when they came to coffin him his
knees were as hard and as stiff to bend as the knees of
a camel. On account of the sternness of his character
he was called James the Just, and James the bulwark
of the people."   Now, in that contemporary account
of James may we not have a clue to the obstinacy
of his unbelief, and to his all but open hostility to
our Lord ?   For James was a Nazarite of such strict-
ness and scrupulosity that he could not fail to be
greatly offended at his Brother's absolute and reso-
lute freedom from all such unspiritual trammels.
James's eldest Brother was no Nazarite.   He was
no Scribe.   He was no Pharisee.   And He must
often have stumbled James, so far did He come
short of a perfect righteousness, as James understood
and demanded perfect righteousness.   In His public
preaching He was compelled to denounce what
James scrupulously practised as the law of Moses
and the law of God.   The Scribes and the Pharisees
were continually finding fault with James's Brother
for His laxity in the traditions of the elders, and
no man would feel that laxity so acutely as James
would feel it.   So rooted was James in the old
covenant that, even after his conversion, he still
continued to cleave fast to his unevangelical habits
of thought and practices of life, in a way and to
an extent that caused the greatest trouble to the
rest of the apostles, and to Paul especially.   In our
Lord's words, James, all his days, was one of those
men, and a leader among them, who continued to
pour the new wine of the gospel into the old bottles
of the law, till the old bottles burst in their hands

and the new wine was spilled. Converted as he undoubtedly was, James was half a Pharisee to the very end. And, if ever he was a bishop at all, he was the bishop of a half-enlightened Jewish ghetto rather than of a Christian church. Still, when all is said, we have an intense interest in James; not so much for his position or for his services in the apostolic church, as for this, that he was the brother, the born and brought-up brother, of our Lord.

James was the born and brought-up brother of our Lord, and, by that, he being dead, yet speaketh. And the one supreme lesson that James teaches us to-night is surely this, 'Keep your eyes open at home, for I made this tremendous mistake. The unpardonable and irreparable mistake of my whole life was this, that my eyes were never opened at home till it was too late. I never once saw what was for thirty years, day and night, staring me in the face, if I had not been stone-blind. It never entered my mind all those years that He was any better than I was myself. Indeed, I often blamed Him that He was not nearly so good as myself. But I remember now: we all remember now, endless instances of His goodness, His meekness, His humility, His lowliness of mind and heart. We often recall to one another how we all took our own way with Him, and got our own way with Him in everything. How silent He was when we were all speaking, and would not hold our peace. How obliging He was, how gentle, how sweet. But, all the time, we saw it not till it was all over, and it was too late.' The kingdom of heaven did not come with sufficient

observation to James. Had his elder Brother been
a Pharisee, had He been a Scribe, had He been a
John the Baptist, had His raiment been of camel's
hair, had His meat been locusts and wild honey,
and had He had His dwelling among the rocks,
James would have found it far easier to believe in
his Brother. But the still small voice of a holy
life at home made no impression on James. Yes:
let us all acknowledge James's tremendous mistake,
and let us all go home with our eyes opened lest
the kingdom of heaven may have come to our own
house also, and we may not see that till it is too
late. A Christian character may be displayed before
our eyes at home, and we may never discover it,
just because it is at home. Ay, and let us beware
of this, lest our hard ways, our proud ways, our
selfish tempers and our want of love, may all be
the daily cross and thorn of some child of God
hidden from our eyes in our own homes, as James
was to Jesus. Out of doors many began to believe
in James's Brother, but no one indoors. In His
own home, and among His own brothers and sisters,
our Lord had no recognition and no honour.

And James is a warning to us all in this respect
also, that he never, to the very end, became a true
and complete New Testament believer. Whether
it was that he had been too long an unbeliever, and
never could make up for the opportunities he had
lost; or whether it was that he yielded to his natural
temper too much, and let it take too deep a hold
of him; or whether it was that he was never able to
suppress himself so as to submit to sit at Paul's

feet; or whether it was that he could never shake off the hard and narrow men who hampered and hindered him; or whether it was his life-long chastisement and impoverishment for neglecting the incomparably glorious opportunity God had given him for thirty-three years,—whatever was the true explanation of it, the fact is only too clear on too many pages of the New Testament, that James, all his days, was far more of a Jew than a genuine Christian. His canonical Epistle itself belongs more to the Old Testament than to the New. Luther felt afterwards that he had gone too far in what he had said in his haste about the Epistle of James. But every one who knows and loves and lives upon Paul's Gospel as Luther did, will sometimes feel something of Luther's mind about James and his Epistle. Though his risen Brother appeared to James as he appeared to Paul, at the same time, God could never be said to have manifested His Son in James as He had manifested Him in Paul. Account for it as we may: brother of our Lord, Bishop of Jerusalem, pillar of that Church as he was and all, James never came within sight of Paul as a New Testament saint of Christ and an evangelical apostle. James never entered himself, and he never led his people, into the glorious liberty of the sons of God. Surely a most solemn warning to us, that our natural tempers, our traditional prejudices, our early sympathies, the school of life and thought and worship in which we have been brought up, and our not ignoble loyalty to that form of doctrine into which we were in our youth delivered,

—all that may stand in our way; all that may have to be fought against and conquered; if we are ever to come in the unity of the faith, and of the knowledge of the Son of God, unto a perfect man, unto the measure of the stature of the fulness of Christ.

Note to the Reader

Volume 2 of the Shepherd Illustrated Classic Edition of *Bible Characters from the New Testament* begins with Stephen and continues through to Timothy, thus concluding Alexander Whyte's useful and inspiring delineations of the personalities and drama of the New Testament.

Dr. Whyte's six-volume series as originally published included three books covering the Old Testament and one entitled *Our Lord's Characters*.